LIFE AND ADVENTURES OF GEORGE NIDEVER

GEORGE NIDEVER

The Life and Adventures of
GEORGE NIDEVER
[1802-1883]

Edited by William Henry Ellison

UNIVERSITY OF CALIFORNIA PRESS
BERKELEY, CALIFORNIA
1937

UNIVERSITY OF CALIFORNIA PRESS
BERKELEY, CALIFORNIA

CAMBRIDGE UNIVERSITY PRESS
LONDON, ENGLAND

COPYRIGHT, 1937, BY THE
REGENTS OF THE UNIVERSITY OF CALIFORNIA

CONTENTS

	PAGE
Acknowledgments	v
Introduction	vii
George Nidever: 1878, by E. F. Murray	xi
Recollections of His Life and Adventures as Dictated by George Nidever to E. F. Murray	1
Notes	91
Bibliography	123
Index	127

ILLUSTRATIONS

	PAGE
George Nidever	*Frontispiece*
Target-shooting by George Nidever at 75 Years	*facing* xi
Sinforosa Sanchez Nidever	*facing* 58
Facsimile of a Page of the Manuscript	90

ACKNOWLEDGMENTS

THANKS ARE DUE the officials of the Bancroft Library for permission to use the Nidever and Dittmann documents and other sources; to Miss Barbara Clark for typing the book; to the editors of the *Pacific Historical Review* for permission to republish, in footnotes, material used in an article therein published; to Dr. George P. Hammond for permission to use the edited section of a part of the Nidever document with a historical introduction that was published in Volume Two of *New Spain and the Anglo-American West;* and to Mr. Samuel T. Farquhar, University Printer, and Mr. Harold A. Small, Editor of the University of California Press, for their courtesies and assistance.

WILLIAM H. ELLISON

Santa Barbara, California,
January 30, 1935.

INTRODUCTION

GEORGE NIDEVER, a pioneer of California from the year 1834, was born on the frontier in East Tennessee in the year 1802. He was the third child in a family of six sons and three daughters, and he outlived all the others. When he was five years old the family moved to Buncombe County, North Carolina. Nine years later a move was made to the Moreau River in Missouri. Four years after the arrival in Missouri, a party including young George Nidever set out for a frontier point on the Six Bull River north of the Arkansas, but, finding that this section had been given over to Cherokee and other Indians, they finally went to the vicinity of Fort Smith. The Nidever family settled here a little later. After George had made a trip to Austin's Grant in Texas, where he did not choose to remain, he settled down with his family near Fort Smith and remained at home from 1822 to 1828.

After he and Alex. Sinclair had given a year to an unsuccessful attempt to build a raft of cedar logs on the Canadian Fork of the Arkansas, which they planned to sell in New Orleans, they decided to take to hunting. In May, 1830, they joined a party of hunters and trappers that was formed just above Fort Smith under the headship of a Colonel Bean. Sinclair, like Nidever, had been reared on the frontier. Both were excellent shots, and because of their skill they became the huntsmen detailed to supply the party with fresh meat and game. The party of forty-eight men went up the North Fork of the Canadian and Arkansas rivers, through the Cross Timbers, into the mountains, and finally made their way down into New Mexico to Arroyo Seco and San Fernando de Taos. On the way they had exciting encounters with numerous bands of Indians. Ten men turned back after the first serious Indian difficulty, two were killed, and at Arroyo Seco Colonel Bean and others left the party, some to return to Arkansas, some to join other companies. Only fifteen men of the original band were left.

The diminished band set out for the Platte in March, 1831, and returned to Arroyo Seco in July. In September they started again, planning to go first to the headwaters of the Arkansas. A few Mexicans and a number of French trappers accompanied them. From the headwaters of the Arkansas they went on to the Platte, where the Mexican and French trappers left them. From the Platte they made their way to the Green River valley, where they went into winter quarters.

In the spring of 1832 the band trapped a little before setting out for the rendezvous in Pierre's Hole. The breakup of the rendezvous was followed by a battle with the Blackfeet Indians in which Sinclair, the devoted friend of Nidever, was killed. The leaderless band hunted through the winter, and in the summer of 1833 Nidever and a few others joined the section of Bonneville's company under Captain Joseph R. Walker that made the famous trip into California across the upper Sierra Nevada.

Nidever began his hunting career in California with George C. Yount in the region of San Francisco Bay, but soon went to Santa Barbara. There he became renowned as a hunter along the coast and on the Channel Islands. Eventually he married a daughter of the country and became identified with its life. Up to the time of the American conquest, his experiences were as varied as they were exciting, whether he was hunting sea otters and grizzly bears, fighting with the northwestern Indians used by American and British sea captains around the Channel

Islands, or campaigning with Frémont, whose company he joined after Frémont reached Santa Barbara in his march south in reconquest of the country.

The gold fields appealed to the adventurous spirit of Nidever, but he had no success with the claim he took up. He acted as pilot for the United States surveyors who made the first surveys in the Channel Island region. One of the most noteworthy of his exploits was the search for and rescue of the "Lone Woman of the Island of San Nicolas." She had lived alone on this island for eighteen years, when she was found and brought ashore to Nidever's home in 1852. From 1860 until his death on March 24, 1883, Nidever lived quietly in Santa Barbara.

In 1878 Edward F. Murray* received the story of Nidever's adventures from the frontiersman's own lips, recording it in a document of one hundred and sixty-five pages, which was read to Nidever and signed by him as correct. The document which follows is the complete Nidever narrative as it was written down by Murray and prepared for publication by the editor. In addition to the human interest of the story, it throws light upon the struggle of

---

* Edward F. Murray was an experienced assistant of Hubert Howe Bancroft, who regarded him as a "faithful and competent man." Before coming to Bancroft, he was engaged for a while in the work of collecting and deciphering historical materials for Judge Benjamin Hayes, who for twenty-five years was an enthusiastic collector and preserver of historical data. Hayes recommended Murray to Bancroft as an expert in the work of deciphering and copying.

When Judge Hayes declined to make an abstract of the archives at Santa Barbara because of professional demands and failing health, the task was assigned to Murray. He began in June, 1876, and continued with few interruptions until the latter part of the year 1878. The results of his work were many large manuscript volumes of mission and other archives, and a number of dictations by old residents. *The Adventures of George Nidever* was one of the last pieces of work done by Murray in Santa Barbara. See H. H. Bancroft, *Literary Industries* (San Francisco, 1890), 478–482, 510–529, for fuller description of Murray as a man and a worker.

frontiersmen with natives and with nature, and gives valuable information on a pioneer activity of marked historical importance. Also, it is a valuable contribution to the history of California in the fifteen years preceding the treaty of Guadalupe Hidalgo.

In a sense, George Nidever is a symbolic figure, a type, for the qualities of initiative, courage, and unswerving integrity possessed by him were likewise possessed in good measure by other pathfinding frontiersmen who pioneered. There were hundreds of men whose lives and experiences were so similar to those of George Nidever that when one writes of him one is writing of them all. Differing in details, in broad outline their lives mark these men as being of the same "tribe," so to speak. Were it possible to recount the story of each of these lives and to tie the stories in with the developments which these lives touched, we should have a true and full history of an important epoch in American life. But most of these heroes of the Rocky Mountains and trail-makers to the Pacific are unknown and unnamed in historical annals; so the original narrative of the life and adventures of George Nidever, a typical figure in a period of American expansion, becomes, as we shall see, both a fascinating and a historically important document.

W. H. E.

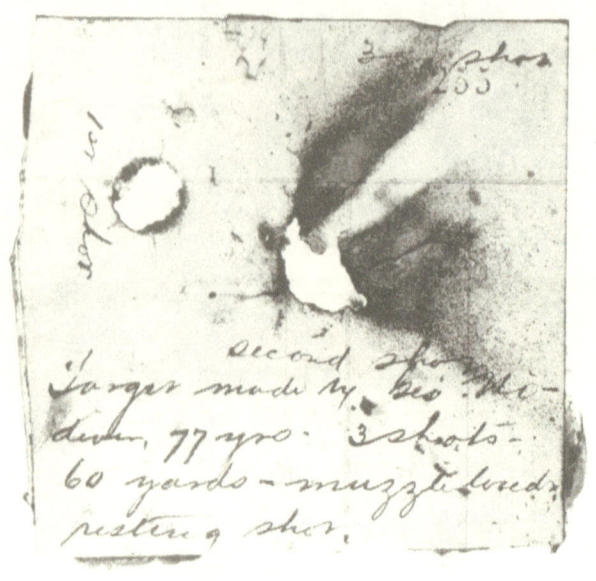

**TARGET-SHOOTING BY GEORGE NIDEVER
AT THE AGE OF 75 YEARS**

GEORGE NIDEVER: 1878

THE SUBJECT of this sketch, although already over 76 yrs. of age,* is still strong and active. He is about the medium height and inclined to be stout. He stoops the least bit but it may be from habit rather than old age. His sight and hearing are still keen and his nerves remarkably steady for one so old. He lives with his youngest daughter and wife, about a mile from town, on a piece of land containing several acres. It is under cultivation and he keeps it free from squirrels by shooting them with a Colt's revolver. If a chicken is wanted for dinner he prefers shooting its head off with his rifle to using a shot gun, which he has frequently to use, however, owing to the danger of using his rifle when there are so many and near neighbors.

Yesterday I induced him to shoot at a target; the result is shown on the opposite page. As will be seen, the second shot hit the nail.

He is quite unassuming and never brags of his feats of skill, and almost everything of this nature relating to him I first learned from others, obtaining a recital of them from him only by dint of questioning. His truthfulness and integrity are beyond question, so that great weight should be given to all he says.†

(Signed) E. F. MURRAY

Santa Barbara Cal[ifornia],
Sept. 1 1878.

---

* Nidever was not 76 until December 20, 1878.

† Stephen Bowers wrote in the *Ventura Observer,* December 20, 1892, that "he [Nidever] was much respected in Santa Barbara, where he lived more than fifty years. We never heard his integrity called in question by anyone."

Recollections of His Life and Adventures as Dictated by George Nidever to E. F. Murray

Recollections of
George Nidever

My name is George Nidever. I was born in 1802, Dec. 20, in Sulivan Co., East Tenn. My father, also named George, was a native of Penn[sylvania].; I do not remember the town. His father died while he was quite young. My father removed to Tenn[essee]. when about 20 yrs. of age. Here he was married to Christina Punkhouser, a native of Virginia, but whose family had removed to Tenn. some years before. My father's business was farming, which he carried on while he lived. Before and after his marriage he took part, as a volunteer, in the early Indian wars with the Cherokees, Shawnees, and other hostile tribes. Besides myself, there were 8 other children; three daughters and five (5) sons. I was third; my two brothers John and Jacob being older than I. Of these none but myself now remain. My oldest brother John[1]* died here in Santa Barbara about five yrs. ago. Jacob died in Arkansas, do not recollect the year, but think it was about 1848. Mark, who followed [me], was killed in Nov. of 1830,[2] at the beginning of my first hunting expedition. Isabella, who came next to Mark, married a man by the name of Harril and died while I was in Arkansas. Henry, the next in age, married a Miss Sinclair, a native of Illinois; (Mark married into the same family). He (Henry) died in Texas

---
* Superior figures refer to notes which will be found at the back of the book.

I think about 1850, leaving a large family. Next came Nancy, she [was] married, after I left home, to a man by the name of Barker; she died in Arkansas, I think, about 1850. Next in order came Daniel, who left home with a party that went down the Mississippi somewhere about 1837 or 8, and was never heard from. Christina, my youngest sister, was drowned in Arkansas.

My family removed, when I was 5 yrs. old, from Sulivan Co., Tenn., to Buncombe Co., N. C. Here we settled down and worked a farm for about 9 years (when I was nearly 14 yrs. of age), when we went to Crawford Co., Mo., and settled on a farm situated on a river called the Moro.[3] Here we followed farming for several years. When I was about 18 (in 1820 or thereabouts), a party of 7 families started through the wilderness for Arkansas, and my brother Jacob and I accompanied them, with a few cattle we took to sell, for the purpose of seeing Arkansas and with the intention of going back for our family if we found the country good.

Among our party there were about twenty men, including my brother and myself, all frontiersmen and a sufficient number to insure protection from the Indian tribes we might encounter. We had no adventure of note during our journey of over two months although we saw many parties of Indians and passed through the country of the Osage Indians.[4] They stole a few of our horses but did not offer to trouble us in any other way.

About half way on our journey our bread gave out and we were obliged to live on meat the rest of the way. The whole country through which we passed was filled with game, so that we never wanted for fresh meat. We had left Mo. in the fall, about the month of Oct., and in December we reached Ark.

His Life and Adventures 3

Our point of destination was the Six Bull river,[6] north of the Arkansas, a locality formerly visited by some members of our party, and where they had decided to make their homes. Two or three months later, however, they were obliged to move south of the Arkansas, owing to this section having been ceded by the Govt. to the Cherokees[6] and other Indians. They finally settled near or in the vicinity of Fort Smith.[7] Among these families there were two or three by the name of Mathers, one Blevin, and one Harril, the same family into which my sister afterwards married.

My brother Jacob sold his stock, consisting of hogs and cattle, to the Choctaw[8] and Cherokee Indians, at a good bargain, and settled down on a farm just below Fort Smith. The next year all of our family came from Mo. and settled a few miles from my brother Jacob's place.

Soon after our party left the Six Bull river for the neighborhood of Fort Smith, I left them for Texas in company with a young man by the name of Daniel Shipman, one of our party from Mo., who, like myself, fond of travel and adventure, and with a desire to see that state, had determined to make a trip through that section of the country.

We went to that portion of Texas then known as Austin's Grant,[9] visited several parts of this tract, and two months later returned to Fort Smith. Shipman soon returned to Texas with his father[10] and mother and several brothers and sisters who had come from Mo. with us.

They begged me to go with them but I had no desire to return at that time.

From 1822 until 1828 I made my home with my family. In 1827, I think, my mother died. In 1828, Alex. Sinclair,[11] a man living near Fort Smith, and I went up the Canadian fork of the Arkansas and began the building of a large raft of cedar logs, which we intended to float down to New Orleans and sell. We were engaged, with a few men we hired, nearly a year in making this raft. When everything was ready, and we were about to start down the river, the Cherokees, to whom that section had been ceded, attempted to seize our raft, but taking advantage of a freshet we sailed down in the night beyond their reach, and escaped them. This availed us but little, however, for, at the mouth of the fork, the raft ran aground, was broken up, and we abandoned it.

This misfortune decided both Sinclair and myself to take to hunting and trapping, so in May of 1830 we joined a party of trappers and hunters that was forming just above Fort Smith. A man by the name of Bean,[12] commonly called Colonel, a native of Tenn., I think, or at least a former resident of that state although he had been living for some time in Ark., was at its head. He was an elderly man and by occupation a gunsmith. He had never had any experience in hunting and trapping, like that which was before us, and, in fact, of our whole party of 48 men but three had fought the Indians and none had ever trapped.

In those days the beaver were, it was supposed, plenty in the streams of the Rocky Mountains and the trapping of them, although attended with great risks owing to the Indians, was largely engaged in by the frontier settlers. Col. Bean was the first to propose the forming of a hunting and trapping expedition, and he had no trouble in raising our party from among the families in the vicinity.

All of our men could handle the rifle and like myself had been brought up to the hunting of small game, although I had already, as some three others, become a good deer and buffalo hunter. Before I was 9 yrs. old I began to use firearms, and being very fond of hunting and shooting at a target I soon became an excellent shot. When I went with the party from Mo., I had already become one of the crack shots at the annual shooting matches in the section where I lived, having but very few equals. This of course encouraged me to greater effort, and with the continual practice the then abundance of game afforded me, I soon became one of the most successful hunters in that portion of the country. Among our party from Mo. there were three of the best hunters detailed to supply the camp with meat, but notwithstanding they were good shots I could always kill three times as much game as any of them, so that ere long I was appointed the chief hunter of the party. This piqued the old hunters not a little, who attempted to attribute the excellence of my shooting to my rifle, but, having exchanged guns with them from time to time, without any apparent change in my shooting, they finally concluded that I could beat them. Our Capt., Harril, had so much confidence in my shooting that he declared I could kill anything if I had only a corncob.

I had also in after years become such a skillful buffalo hunter that on several occasions companies of trappers among the mountains offered to bet as high [as] $5000 that I could kill more buffalo than any other man in the Rocky Mountains.

Sinclair, my partner in the building of the raft, was a very good shot and buffalo hunter, having been raised on the Western Frontier. He had also done considerable Indian fighting. He could not travel much on foot, owing to the loss of the toes and part of the left foot, in what manner I do not recollect. He was then about 40 yrs. of age. A younger brother of about 30 also formed one of our party; he was no hunter and but a very ordinary shot.

While in the mountains I was as a general rule detailed to supply the party with fresh meat, and, as game abounded throughout our whole journey to the mountains, I was always successful.

Each man was to equip himself and hunt for himself, except that we were to keep together in moving about, for mutual protection, or, as it afterward happened, several men or messes, of six men each, would form a company, dividing equally the skins.

The equipment of each man was rifle and six traps. Besides this, most of the men had a pistol, knife, and a small hatchet that could be conveniently carried in the belt. We had the best of ammunition. For convenience in cooking, &c, we were divided into messes of six men each, one of each mess usually volunteering to do the cooking, preferring it to hunting, and he of course received his share of pelts. My equipment was the same as that of the others excepting my pistol which I had ordered made. It was the same bore as my rifle, and it would kill a buffalo at 40 yds.

Our intention was, when we set out, to be gone about a year or 18 months. We left the vicinity of Fort Smith in May 1830, and followed up the north fork of the Canadian and the Arkansas rivers until we struck the Rocky Mountains, and from there across into New Mexico. We had procured a map and with its aid we made our way with little trouble.

When we started we had, each, two pack animals and some three, so that we travelled slowly, and, besides, frequent freshets kept us back. About the first of July we reached the Cross Timbers[12] about two hundred miles from Fort Smith.

But just here I may as well give you the names of our company that I can remember. First came Col. Bean our

Captain, whom we had elected rather because he had always borne a good name among us and was very much esteemed, than from any superior skill or knowledge he possessed in affairs relating to the control and management of such a expedition, besides being older than most of us. He was accompanied by a son, a young man about 24 yrs. of age. Two men by name of Green, although not related; Basey, a large powerful man; he would probably weigh at least 240 lbs; Carmichael, who was afterwards treacherously killed by a Mexican here in Cal[ifornia]. during one of the revolutions; Bowen; Saunders, an old man; Allen, who I think is still living, in Los Angeles Co.; Baldwin, one of our best shots; Williams; Frazier, who also came to Cal.; Weaver, who also came to Cal.; Graham, of whom I shall have more to say hereafter; Tom Hammonds; Anderson; Hace who left us in New Mexico in 1831 between June and Sept.; Mark, my brother; Price, and Potter.[14] These are all the names I can recollect at present, but in the course of my story will no doubt be able to recall those of some of the others.

From the Cross Timbers we continued our course towards the mountains, making very slow marches.

About the latter part of Aug. or first of Sept., having marched some 200 to 250 miles since leaving the Cross Timbers, six of us started out one afternoon to hunt buffalo. We had been for several days travelling in a country frequented by Comanches,[15] but had seen no signs of them, and had taken no other precautions on the march than to keep close together, sometimes riding by twos and sometimes four abreast when the country was open and level. No one was especially detailed to keep a lookout, for the air was so clear that objects could be seen at a very great distance. I frequently saw buffalo as far as 9 miles away, making them out without any difficulty. I have never been in any place since, nor before, where the air seemed so remarkably clear. Then we always rode close together so that within fifteen minutes after an alarm we could have been prepared to receive an enemy. At night, too, ever since entering the Indian country, we formed our packs into a circular breastwork, with our horses picketed inside, and a guard of from three to five, sometimes more, relieved every four (4) hours, throughout the night. Our party of six, having left the camp, separated; three keeping in close to the edge of the belt of timber that ran along the river, the other three, and among them myself, taking the open and higher ground some distance from and opposite the first three. We rode along for some distance in our relative positions, without discovering any buffalo. At last the party skirting the timber saw some horse in the distance, grazing near the edge of the timber, and with the hopes of capturing them, for they naturally thought them wild horses, they approached them under cover. Their surprise as well as alarm, however, can be imagined when, upon nearing the animals, they discovered them to be tied. They immediately started at full speed towards us and, hardly five minutes after, two Comanche Indians emerged from the timber, on horseback, and rode after our companions. Following these came others until they were, I should judge, about forty altogether. We ran and they followed us, and, being better mounted than we were, soon came within shooting distance. They discharged a shower of arrows at us, many of them going beyond us. We saw that it was useless to run any farther, so stood our ground, or, rather, rode leisurely towards camp. They did not offer to attack us, but one of them, more daring than the rest, charged down on us alone and rode near enough to throw his lance, which was easily dodged. We supposed that he would ride directly by us and as shots are always uncertain when fired at an object in such rapid motion, we would have let him pass, but instead of doing this he rode off at right angles to our party, in a perfectly straight line, and, loth to lose such a chance, I drew bead on him and tumbled him out of his saddle, and some of our boys caught his horse. This brought forth a yell from the Indians, who, however, did not trouble us any more. Upon reaching camp we wanted to take half of our men and go back and attack the Indians, but Col. Bean refused, to the great dissatisfaction of all of the party, who from his ways had already lost some confidence in him and now they suspected, and with reason as will be seen hereafter, that he was not over brave.

At this juncture ten (10) of our party left us, declaring their intention to go back to Arkansas, as they feared to go into Indian country with Bean as Capt. I have never heard what became of them.

In the hopes of avoiding the Indians we decided a day or two after to leave the North Fork and go over to the Arkansas. Our course had lain chiefly along the north bank of the North Fork. The country we had come through was very fine, the land rich, well timbered, especially near the river, and game in abundance. We travelled very leisurely, making on an average from 15 to 20 miles a day, striking camp about 7 or 8 o'clock in the morning usually, and pitching camp again all the way from 3 to 5 in the afternoon. During the early part of our journey we were frequently delayed by swollen streams, and occasionally by the illness of some of the men, which would make it necessary to halt a day or two.

As had been decided, we went over to the Arkansas

River[16] and having reached it crossed to its northern side. This river we intended to follow until we should reach the mountains. A day or two later, in the early part of the afternoon we came upon several Pawnee[17] warriors, who came out from the timber to meet our party, and others joined us as we marched along until they numbered all told about 80. About half of them were mounted. They were a war party as they had no women with them; a few had rifles but the majority had only bows and arrows. They were fine looking Indians, about the medium height but well made and active. Their dress was the customary buckskin leggings and the breech clout; a few had shirts. Upon first seeing us they made signs of friendship, but although we considered them friendly Indians we did not place much confidence in their good will. Our leader, however, was very generous with them, making them presents of blankets, tobacco, and even knives and powder, which the most of our party very much disapproved of.

It must have been about 2 o'clock in the afternoon when we met the Pawnees, and soon after we went into camp. They went into camp also about 60 yds. from us, in the same body of timber. The next morning we moved on and left them, and the next afternoon camped about the usual hour.

Having to do most of the hunting, I usually started out as soon as we got into camp, and generally took my brother Mark with me while he lived. Sometimes others accompanied me, as a rule either Isaac Graham[18] or my old companion Alex. Sinclair.

This afternoon I started out with Graham, to get buffalo, if possible.

We went fully four miles from camp before we saw anything; then we saw the objects of our search at a distance.

We were on foot, so had little trouble in approaching them, but before we got within range I saw an Indian's head peeping out of a hollow, and I at once saw that we had been drawn into a trap. I at once told Graham, and we took to our heels immediately, with a party of 80 Arapahoes close behind. Two of them only were mounted, but the rest of them were good runners and our chances of saving our scalp[s] was very small. We were out in the open country, the nearest timber being that of the river belt, fully a mile and a half away, and a pack of fleet footed red skins close upon us. We saw that our only hope was to reach the timber where perhaps we might be able to defend ourselves.

Graham was a good runner, the best in fact in our party, and had he wished could soon have left me in the rear, but it was not his character to desert a comrade in danger, so we kept together straining every nerve to reach the shelter of the woods. The Indians on horseback of course gained on us at once, and we were obliged to turn alternately and by aiming at them check them for a moment. Under any other circumstances it would have been amusing to see the horsemen make their horses jump quickly from side to side, at the same time throwing their own bodies this way then that to prevent our taking aim at them when we raised our rifles, but we only realized that each stoppage was enabling those on foot, who were steadily pressing forward, to gain ground. The chase had been kept up nearly a mile, I should judge, when our pursuers were so close upon us that we had determined to fire on them. Graham, although naturally a brave man, was not a little frightened and was almost exhausted by our long run, so that in his fright he did not see the foremost Indians throw down their guns when he turned to fire, but

I fortunately did and thus prevented his shooting, as good fortune would have it. Had he shot, he would undoubtedly have killed one and perhaps more, for he would have fought to the last, but however many we might have killed, numbers would have overpowered us, and I would not be here to tell about it nor [would] Graham have become famous as leader of the riflemen in Cal[ifornia]. As soon as the Indians came up to us, they took hold of us and shook us roughly, and finally made us sit down on the ground while they seated themselves in a circle around us. They lit their pipe and passed it around, holding council for some time, no doubt about what should be done with us. By signs we tried to make them understand that we slept with 80 whites the night before not far from them, hoping this might induce them to spare our lives. It had the desired effect, for they soon got up and made motions that we too should get up and lead them to our camp. We needed no second bidding but took the direction of camp with our captors. We soon reached our party, to our great relief, and the Arapahoes camped near us. Our men had not suspected anything when they saw us coming in with the Indians, supposing that they were friendly to us. That night we doubled our guard and took every precaution to prevent a surprise. The night before we had done the same to guard against surprise from our Pawnee friends and there was good cause for it, for they were prowling around our camp all night, and only the fact that we were on the alert and prepared, prevented them from attacking us.

   The Arapahoes had gone into camp at about the same distance from us as the Pawnees the night previous. I was on guard until twelve o'clock at night, and several times had seen Indians prowling about that did not appear to me to be Arapahoe Indians, and upon being relieved by Price I told him and cautioned him to keep a good lookout. It was not long before he saw an Indian approaching his post, whereupon he called out, "Who's that?" His answer was the snap of a gun lock and the flash of a flint. The Indian's gun did not go off, but Price's did, and we heard afterwards that an Indian was killed. At Price's shot, a yell arose on all sides of us and those who were on guard knew that the Pawnees were on us, as the Arapahoe camp had been perfectly quiet. Alex. Sinclair, who was also on guard, called out, "Help, boys." We were all on our feet in an instant and our arms, which we always kept at our sides, ready for use. The Indians fired a discharge of arrows and a few shots among us, but did no further damage than to wound a few horses. We replied to their shots but as the night was dark we could not shoot with any certainty, for we could aim only when we saw the flash of their guns. We thought the Arapahoes also fired a few shots among us, but it was not positively known. We had a small cannon with us and having loaded it with 60 bullets we discharged it in the direction of our enemies, and succeeded in silencing their fire. We passed the rest of the night waiting for their return, but morning came and they had disappeared, and our friends the Arapahoes left us at an early hour. As a result of the night attack we found that we had lost 7 horses stolen, and as many more wounded. With the beginning of the firing, our brave Col. Bean had been lost sight of, as also a man by the name of Williams. They became frightened and hid themselves. From that time Col. Bean was totally disregarded and hardly treated civilly so that, soon after, when we got into New Mexico, he went to San Fernando and finally returned to Ark. with the first train of the regular traders that went back.[19] Alex. Sinclair was by tacit agreement looked up to as our leader and continued in command until he was killed.[20] He was a good leader although a trifle easy.

The Arapahoes were all good looking Indians, somewhat larger than the Pawnees and armed and dressed about the same.

The country we had come through abounded in buffalo and wild horses. The former roamed in immense herds. I have never seen so many cattle in my life as I saw buffalo in that country. Wild horses were frequently captured by shooting them through the neck just above the spine, usually called creasing. This knocked them down, when the hunter would catch them before they could regain their feet. The wound healed soon, and with a little training the horse soon became manageable.

Our meat was principally buffalo, although we occasionally killed deer and bear. In the Cross Timber, on the N. Fork there was abundance of turkeys and of wild honey.

The next morning after the Pawnees attacked us, we left our camp soon after the Arapahoes did theirs. Two days' travel brought us to the Indian village of our captors, where we remained over night. This village contained about 200 or 250 warriors and perhaps as many women and children. We passed a sleepless night, and were rejoiced to leave our red friends behind the next morning at an early hour. From this point we had but 150 miles to go to reach the mountains. This we accomplished in about a week. Arrived at the foot of the Mts., we found plenty of feed and our party went into camp. Six of us were sent forward to examine the country before us, and to search for a passable trail; as also feed for our animals.

Here we saw for the first time the black-tail deer. There were large numbers of them, so that we had no trouble in killing a considerable quantity for their meat, which we hung up to await the arrival of the main party. We slept one night in the Mts. and the following morning started back to camp. On the way, however, Dr. Craig, one of our party, gave out, so that Price and I were obliged to remain with him while the other three went to bring our party up. Before night they had returned with the rest of our company and we went into camp near where we had hung up the deer's meat. Here too, the feed was quite plenty [plentiful] and it was decided to remain for a few days to allow the animals to recruit. From this place another advance party of six was sent out, to cross the mountains and proceed as far as the head waters of the Arkansas.

My brother Mark, a man by the name of Crist, Graham, Basey, Dye, and I, were of the party. We arrived at our journey's end without any adventure and camped in a beautiful valley in which the buffalo abounded and feed was plenty. We immediately set to work to kill buffalo and soon had the satisfaction of seeing a large quantity, hung up out [of] the reach of the wolves and coyotes, ready for the coming of those behind.

As soon as this was done two of our party, Mark and Crist, went back to camp to report, while we, who remained, removed our camp from the edge of the valley, where we had hung the buffalo meat, about two miles away and up the mountain's side. From this point we had a full view of the valley below, while our camp was hidden from those who might pass through the valley. From a small rise near our camp, we could at all times see our buffalo meat. This change of camp was made to guard against surprise from the Indians. In an Indian country one cannot take too many precautions, and I owe my life many times over to my habitual vigilance and caution in all my movements while in the mountains. Of the many trappers I have known that were killed in the mountains by Indians, a very large proportion of them were careless and imprudent in their habits. When out with a small force, I invariably ate supper and remained until dark in one place, and as soon as night came on moved away some distance to sleep.

We had been in our new camp but a few days when, having gone out on the rise to look towards our meat, I saw a war party of Arapahoes, of perhaps 80 or more, engaged in taking it down. This decided us to leave that dangerous neighborhood with all possible haste and make our way back to the rest of our party. About half way back we met our companions at a former camp of the war party of the Arapahoes I had discovered seizing our buffalo meat. They had arrived there but a few hours before and the first objects that met their sight were the dead bodies of Mark, my brother, and Crist.[n] They were scalped, and stabbed in several places. From our party we learned that our two dead comrades had arrived safely at the camp, informed them where we were, and started back to find us. We were never able to find out the manner in which they were killed, but from some Mexicans to whom the Arapahoes sold their guns afterwards, we gleaned the following facts. The party that chased and captured Graham and me understood from the signs we made that there were 80 more white men back in the direction we pointed. The fear of being punished by these 80 white men, should they kill us, no doubt induced them to spare our lives. When they reached our camp, however, and found only 36 men, they at once concluded that the rest were coming up, and sent some of their best runners back to find them. These runners did not return until our party was already in the mountains. They reported having seen no more white men, whereupon a war party was immediately sent out to overtake and attack us. They fell in with my brother and Crist, who, probably recognizing them as the same that had camped with us before and through whose village we passed, and unsuspicious, travelled along with them, until an opportunity offered and the Indians killed them. Of the precise circumstances immediately connected with their death, the Mexicans knew nothing, other than that my brother had killed 3 of the Indians before they killed him.

Crist was a quiet inoffensive man, but little versed in mountain life and with no skill in the use of arms.

My brother, on the contrary, was one of the best men we had in our company—active, strong, hardy, brave, and a good shot. He was missed and mourned by all. This sad event led us to turn our course towards New Mexico, considering this section too dangerous for [carrying on any farther] our trapping operations.

During our journey from Fort Smith to the head of the Arkansas we found a few beaver, and at this time had collected about 40 or 50 skins.

As the country through which we must pass before reaching the settlements in New Mexico was almost destitute of grass for our animals, already somewhat reduced, we concluded to hide some of our traps, and having found a deep water hole, threw in about 60 or 70.

After entering New Mexico and just before we reached Arroyo Seco, a small Mexican town and our point of destination, we met the first signs of civilization, in a herd of tame cattle which we saw quietly grazing off to the right of our line of march; soon after, we met a band of sheep driven by a young Mexican on horse back.

When we struck the head of the band they parted, allowing us to ride in among them and without showing any fear at our presence. Not so with their herder, whose attention being diverted did not discover our presence until we were quite close to him, and then with a startled glance saw only that a party of horsemen were upon him, his fright preventing him from distinguishing us. He uttered a yell and put off for the neighboring mountains as fast as his horse could carry him. He took us for a war party of the Arapahoes, as these Indians made frequent incursions into New Mexico in those times. The Arapahoes and Mexicans were deadly enemies, and although they would trade freely with each other, woe betide the poor Mexican who was caught by these savages, and the Mexicans spared no Arapahoe who might fall into their hands.

A few miles farther on we came to a shepherd's hut, its sole occupants an old man and a boy. The old man was the first to see us and he, like the young herder, took us for Arapahoes.

He gave us one look and turning ran at the top of his speed to a ravine near by. He was some distance from the hut and had no time to call to the boy. By this time we were close to the hut, when the boy, hearing us, came out, and recognizing us as white men advanced towards us and held out his hand, showing great pleasure at seeing us. The old man had by this time reached the opposite side of the ravine where he stopped to look back and seeing this boy among us, and realizing that we could not be Indians, he came back almost as fast as he had run away. He ran up to us, caught hold of our hands, and could hardly contain himself with joy. He proceeded to kill a

His Life and Adventures

sheep for us, and brought us out milk and corn cakes, which we ate with the greatest of relish.

Arroyo Seco was about 50 miles distant and we arrived there three days later.[22] Here as at the shepherd's hut, we were received very hospitably, and, in fact, every where in New Mexico, we always met with the same treatment. This seemed to be a great wheat country, and flour was in consequence quite cheap. Upon our arrival at Arroyo Seco they brought us a cart load of bread. There were quite a number of flour mills, also, in and around Arroyo Seco.

About 12 miles from Arroyo Seco was situated the town of San Fernando,[23] quite a large place. The fur traders who came out annually from St. Louis had permanent trading posts established here. We went to Sn. Fernando very often but made our headquarters at Arroyo Seco. Having arrived here our party separated, but 14 or 15 of the original company remaining together.

Those who left us here, as far as I can remember, were,— Col. Bean,[24] who by this time was looked upon by all the company as the most insignificant among us. We had made a great mistake in choosing him for our leader, but the high estimation in which he was held by all, and his rank of Col[onel]. of Militia, led us to suppose him the best man. His brothers were well known to my family, my father having been with them in the early Indian wars. They owned the salt works on the Ark. and were men of good standing.

William Bean also left us here with his father. He was a quiet, sensible young man, with none of his father's cowardice, and was very much liked by all. They both returned to Ark. with the first annual trading train that left San Fernando.[25] Dr. Craig[26] went into Sonora. About

8 or 10 joined Young's[27] party at San Fernando and came to Cal. by the lower route, via Fort Yuma. Among these were Austin, a wild young fellow; Weaver; Hace, Wilkinson; the two Greens, Anderson, and Basey. The names of the others I do not remember. Anderson[28] was killed by one of the Greens,[29] not far from Los Angeles and just after they had entered Cal. While with us, Anderson, who was a large man, had imposed to a great extent upon Green, who was a small man, by continually throwing his [Green's] traps into the river and setting his own on Green's beaver signs. Green had warned him that, if he continued to treat him in that manner, he would certainly kill him. To this threat, however, Anderson paid no heed, nor to the repeated warnings of others of the company, that Green would carry his threat into execution.

He continued to ill treat him until Green put an end to him.

Near the place where he killed Anderson, he had set his traps for beaver, when Anderson, having come across them, threw them into the water, as he had repeatedly done before, and set his own traps in their place. Shortly after, Green visited his traps and, finding Anderson's, returned quietly to camp, walked up to him, and shot him through the heart. Capt. Young gave Green up to the authorities at Los Angeles, but nothing was done with him, I believe, and he was allowed to leave the country.[30]

Dr. Craig[31] is now living in San Francisco and came to see me about 7 or 8 years ago, stopping at my house for several days.

Among those of our party who were left, were the two Sinclairs; Graham; Price; Pollum, a Virginian; Nale [Naile]; and myself; the other names I do not remember.

At San Fernando, Rowland and Workman[32] (of the La

Puente Ranch, Los Angeles Co.) were living; they had already been there, I think, nearly 15 years. Rowland had a flour mill in that town. He was married to a Mexican woman and then had 3 or 4 children. I was well acquainted with the family, having often visited their house while I was in San Fernando. With Workman I had less acquaintance. I was told that he, too, was married to a Mexican woman, but I never visited his house. They afterwards removed to Cal. and settled in Los Angeles Co. Workman had a store in San Fernando. He sold clothing, provisions, &c. We did most of our trading with him. Besides these foreigners, there were the two brothers Kincaid and an old man by the name of Chambers living in San Fernando.

Our party had arrived at Arroyo Seco early in March of '31. A few weeks later, Graham, Sinclair (Alex.), and I decided to make an attempt to get the traps we had left on the Ark. Having secured the services of three Mexicans with their mules and procured fresh animals for ourselves, we lost no time in starting on our trip. A few days brought us within a short distance of our traps, but we found the snow still too deep on the mountains that lay between us and the river. At the same time an event occurred that caused us to retrace our steps with all possible haste. This was the presence in the vicinity of a large party of Arapahoes. We discovered them on a neighboring hill early one morning while we were in camp. Fortunately they did not see us, and as soon as possible we packed up and made our way back to New Mexico, travelling day and night until we were well out of the Indian country. The Mexicans who accompanied us were very much frightened when they saw the Indians and needed no urging to keep up with us in our retreat. We were somewhat disappointed in our failure to get the traps, as they were very dear at San Fernando.

Having sold the few skins we brought with us on our first arrival, we laid in a few supplies and in March ['31], our whole party now reduced to 14 or 15 men, set out for the Platte. On the North Fork we found a valley with beaver and here we remained until we trapped them out. On July 4 of '31, we arrived at Arroyo Seco again with about two packs of skins of 60 each. These we sold in San Fernando, at $4 per pound, or an average of $10 per skin. In those days, although there was a heavy duty on all beaver skins bro't into New Mexico, no one ever thought of paying [on] them and, as in our case, they would be smuggled into town in the night.

We fitted ourselves out a second time and in Sept. 1831 again started for the head waters of the Arkansas. Our party had been increased by the addition of 3 or 4 Mexicans, who had been hired by different members of our company. From Arroyo Seco to the Ark. we kept company with a band of trappers composed of French and Mexicans, about a doz. in all. On our way we saw a few Crow Indians,[33] and had several horses stolen by them. We also saw numbers of the Snake Indians,[34] who were then very friendly towards the *Pale faces*.

Just before we reached the Ark. our camp was alarmed one night by the appearance in our midst of a young Indian woman of the Snake tribe.

An old Mexican who was sleeping near me was awakened in the night by some one passing near him, and reaching out his hand caught hold of her and held her fast, calling out at the same time, "I got one woman." We were all on our feet in an instant and with our arms in our hands ready to meet the expected attack, but no more Indians appeared. We gave the poor woman plenty to eat and the next day she left us for her village not far away. We were able to learn that she had made her escape from the Kiowas,[35] who had taken her prisoner, and had found the buffalo road which ran through our camp and followed it until she was caught in our midst.

She had passed our guard without being seen.

We reached the head waters of the Ark. in Oct. without any further adventure. A few days more brought us to the "Platte."

At this point the Mexican and French trappers left us, going South, down the Platte, while we crossed over to the Green River. Here we went into winter quarters in Nov. We had found a few beaver between the Ark. and Green rivers and had nearly a hundred when we went into our quarters for the winter. Buffalo we had found very scarce, but among the timber in the mountains an abundance of elk. The place we had selected for our winter quarters was a large deep valley on the Green River about 10 miles wide and 20 in length, and opening into a valley on the north and into another on the south.[36] In this valley snow seldom fell and even then never remained. There was usually food for animals all the year around for when the grass grew scarce, or failed, the bark of the sweet cottonwod tree, of which there were immense quantities, supplied its place. This valley was a favorite wintering place both of the whites and Indians. There was always buffalo in the valley so that we seldom wanted for meat.

We remained here three months during which time we were confined to our valley by deep snows that everywhere surrounded it. We had nothing to occupy ourselves with, except the hunting of game for our supply of meat. About

March of '32, we started out of the valley and followed the river towards its head, with the intention of trapping that season on the head waters of the Columbia. We trapped as we went along up the Green River until May, when we learned that the place we intended going was already being trapped by other companies, whereupon we decided not to go there.[37] The party now disagreed as to where we should go, and finally separated, some going in one direction and some another,[38] although the majority went together towards the Platte. At this place we met a trader by the name of O'Felon, an Irishman, who with a half doz. mules had brought liquor and a few articles such as blankets, &c., to trade with the trappers. He was accompanied by a trapper by the name of Harris, and had 6 or 7 Mexicans to attend to his mules and packs. He was bound for Pierre's Hole,[39] a deep valley situated between the Lewis and Henry's Forks, and the appointed rendezvous of the trappers and traders for that year. This would take place in July, so I determined to accompany O'Felon.

We arrived at Pierre's Hole just before the 4th of July [1832]. On our way we had crossed several mountains, and the last one just before reaching Pierre's Hole. Morning found us wading through the snow on its top and by evening we were in the midst of green grass and summer weather at its foot. At Pierre's Hole we found already arrived some 50 or more hunters and trappers. A few days later, a company of 150 trappers under Wm. Sublette arrived from St. Louis bringing supplies.[40] The second in command, Fitzpatrick, they had lost while crossing Green River. Having gone in advance to reconnoitre, he was cut off by the Indians and so hard pressed that he was obliged to abandon his horse and take to the rocks. His companions supposed him killed.

His Life and Adventures   25

A week or so after the arrival of the company, a trapper by name of Poe and I went out for a short hunt, and met Fitzpatrick crossing the Lewis Fork. He was mounted, having by the merest chance caught a horse saddled and bridled, that had escaped from one of the men at Pierre's Hole and wandered to where he was found by Fitzpatrick. Fitzpatrick was shoeless, hatless, and almost naked. In crossing a river his powder horn was lost, and this rendered useless his gun and pistols, which he threw away. For ten days or thereabouts he had wandered about, having in that time eaten of no food excepting a very small piece of dried meat. We piloted him back to camp.[41]

Other hunters, singly and by small companies, continued to arrive at the rendezvous until they numbered in all about 500.[42] This was the favorite rendezvous for trappers West of the Rocky Mts. and had been the center of a rich beaver country. At this time, however, it was well nigh trapped out. The companies then at the rendezvous were, as near as I can remember, William Sublette's,[43] of 150 men—they had come out expressly for trading purposes and returned with about 100 men to St. Louis when the rendezvous broke up; Milton Sublette's,[44] a brother of Wm., composed of about 30 men; Frapp's[45] company, also about 30 men; Wyatt's [Wyeth's] company[46] of emigrants of about 12 to 16, who were going to the mouth of the Columbia to explore [the] country; Perkin's company of about 3 to 5 men.[47]

Our own company had also got together again, making some 14 or 15 more. When we separated on the Green River,[48] the majority of them finally agreed to make a hunt on the Platte River, but having found the country filled with Indians and lost one of their men by them, they turned back. The rest of the trappers at the rendezvous were a class that hunted singly in parts of the Mts. free from the Indians, or in unorganized bands and with no recognized leader; many of these men never leaving the mountains. At the yearly rendezvous they would exchange their pelts for what few supplies they required and then return to the mountains."

About the beginning of Aug. the trappers began to leave for their respective hunting grounds.[50] Our party had decided to trap that season on the Marys River,[51] a small stream about South West of Salt Lake. We left Pierre's Hole in company with Frapp and Wyatt, our courses being the same for some distance.[52] Frapp's company was mostly made up of Canadian French half-breeds. Our first camp was about 15 miles from the rendezvous. Frapp's and Wyatt's companies camped together, while we were a short distance in their rear.

The next morning about 8 o'clock we packed up and rode along to Wyatt's and Frapp's camp, only a few hundred yards ahead, and had hardly reached it when Indians were discovered coming towards us in large numbers, and we immediately recognized them as Blackfeet. They belonged to a village of some 400 warriors or more, that with their women, children, and camp baggage were moving north.[53] They had discovered us before we did them, no doubt, and had resolved on attacking us. They were riding down on us at full speed and barely gave us time to prepare for them. We hurriedly formed a breastwork of our packs and despatched a young boy on our fleetest horse back to Pierre's Hole for aid. We saw from their numbers that we would need help, but by holding the Indians in check for two or three hours we knew reinforcements would reach us. As soon as the Indians arrived within range they began shooting, to which we replied.⁵⁴ Conspicuous among them was a chief dressed in a bright scarlet coat, and he rode somewhat in advance of his men, who began to scatter and surround us upon arriving within shooting distance. On came the chief and out rode one of Wyatt's men, Goddar [Godin], a Canadian half-breed, to meet him. Across his saddle Goddar carried a short rifle which the chief did not see until, when within 40 or 50 yds. of him, Goddar raised it and shot. The chief fell from his saddle dead, and before his companions could come up to him his coat was stripped off by Goddar who amidst a heavy fire reached our camp in safety with his trophy.⁵⁵ We continued to exchange shots, with a loss to the Indians of one or two killed, and to us of several wounded, until about ten o'clock, when the Indians suddenly took shelter in the heavy narrow belt of woods that lay between us and the river. We soon discovered the cause of this unexpected movement, in the coming of our reinforcements, that began to appear in sight and a few minutes later were among us to the number of about 250. Most of them were without saddles, having lost no time in setting out as soon as our messenger reached them. A council was held and Wm. Sublette was elected as our leader. Many were opposed to attacking them as, being posted in the heavy timber, we would find it difficult to drive them out, and our loss would be considerable. These objections were overruled by Sublette and others, who said we would have to fight them anyway and now that we had them at a disadvantage, we must profit by it.

The plan of attack was formed and the attacking party got into line, and advanced, when the firing at once became general. Just after we entered the timber, our captain Alex. Sinclair was shot in the thigh,⁵⁶ Phelps, a man who joined us at Pierre's Hole, was wounded in about the same place, and Wm. Sublette was shot in the arm. Our attacking party did not consist of much over 100 men, the rest refusing to join us. As we advanced and drove the Indians towards the river, the wings of our line gradually turned in until they rested on its bank and we had them surrounded."

Upon penetrating into timber we found that the Blackfeet had constructed a fort of logs on the bank of the river in the form of a half moon, the rear opening towards the river. We continued to advance, dodging and crawling from tree to tree and log to log, every foot stubbornly contested by the redskins, until almost sunset. Some of our men had succeeded in getting in the rear of the fort, which, however, afforded its inmates some shelter even on the open side, as it was filled with trees. One of the trappers of Frapp's company got very near the rear of the fort, almost up to it in fact, by crawling flat on the ground and pushing and rolling a large log so as to protect his head.

Several shots struck the log but the trapper got into the [rear] position and abandoned his log for a tree without being harmed.

Another one of Frapp's men, a Canadian half-breed, tried to distinguish himself by rashly crawling up to the very wall of the fort and then peeping over the top. He paid for his temerity with his life. He had barely raised his head above the breastworks of logs when he received two bullets in his forehead. He was half drunk at the time, liquor having been distributed among the men during the early part of the fight. By sunset we had got so close to the fort that we determined to set it on fire, but before doing so it was agreed to give the Indians a chance to surrender. Accordingly, a renegade Blackfoot who was among Frapp's men was instructed to talk with them and

His Life and Adventures

try and induce them to surrender. They refused, however, and answered that, although they would all be killed that day, the next day it would be our turn, as they had sent word to a very large village of their nation, situated only a short distance from there, numbering some 1500 lodges.[58]

It was well known that there was a very large village nearby, and that, should they send out all of their force after us, there would be some heavy fighting in which we would in all probability get worsted. Upon hearing the answer of the Indians, Frapp became alarmed and withdrew his men at once and this obliged the rest of us to retire, and those from Pierre's Hole having returned, we travelled on about 9 miles and went into camp with the same companies as the night previous. The next morning several of us went back to the scene of the fight. Within the fort and its immediate vicinity the ground was strewn with dead bodies mostly of women and children; but a very few warriors among them.

We counted 50 dead bodies, and inside of the fort were the bodies of 20 fine horses. Of the from 300 to 400 Indians which it was calculated the fighting men of the Blackfeet numbered, but very few escaped.[59]

At the beginning of the engagement several got away, many of them being shot in attempting to swim the river. We afterwards learned through the Indians that when we withdrew our men only 6 Indians were left alive in the fort. The dead Indians were thrown into the river to prevent them from falling into our hands.

Many of the women were shot unintentionally as in the timber it was impossible to distinguish the women from the men; the children were killed no doubt by stray shots.

The Indians make a very poor fight on foot, their usual mode of fighting being to lay [lie] in ambush or to cut off small detached parties with such numbers as to make success sure.

We lost no time in getting out of this neighborhood, pushing forward as rapidly as possible. A few days later we struck buffalo and halted to get meat. We also furnished meat to Wyatt, whose men were mostly green in these matters.

Having got a sufficient supply we continued our journey without further adventure. We parted with Wyatt's company about 100 miles from Pierre's Hole and with Frapp just north of Salt Lake.[60] We trapped on the Marys River with fair success until Oct., when we went North intending to winter in the Green River valley where we had passed the previous winter. We found it already occupied by some of the Snake Indians,[61] and buffalo very scarce so that we determined upon making no permanent quarters but [to] move about from place to place.[62] We visited the head waters of the Red[63] and Yellowstone rivers and trapped a few beavers between the Green and Platte rivers. The cold was very severe. When up near the head waters of the Yellowstone we had several horses stolen by the Indians, and knowing with almost a certainty that the Crow[64] were the thieves, we visited their villages in the hopes of recovering our property, but unsuccessfully offered them a reward to return them.

A white man by the name of Ballard was living among the Crow Indians and served as interpreter. It was rumored that he was a fugitive from justice. During the same winter we met a party of 40 Crow Indians. Their number emboldened them, so that they acted very saucily. One of them, a large powerful fellow, took a fancy to my powder horn. He made signs for me to give it to him, and upon being refused he took out his knife and was about to cut the string with which it was hung from my shoulder and take it. I had my hand on the handle of my knife and was determined to kill him the moment he cut the string; at the same time I called out to our men to look out for themselves. Our Capt. spoke some Crow tongue and warned the Indian, who immediately desisted from his design, all of our men having at that time laid hold of their rifles. The Indians saw that we meant to fight them if necessary and they wisely let us alone.

This nation is one of the most thieving nations of all those that live in the mountains. We lost several horses by them and were never able to find any of them.

In April of the following year we went into the waters of the North Fork of the Platte.⁶⁵ Here we encamped and had our horses picketed a few hundred yards away. One morning, having gone out with a companion to bring in horses, we discovered a band of something like 80 Rees⁶⁶ Indians, riding down on us. We had barely time to get back to camp before the Indians reached the stock, which they immediately drove off. Here a man by the name of Gillum was, it was supposed, killed by these Indians. He had a very fine horse picketed out in another direction and, contrary to all advice, persisted in going for it. We never found him again.⁶⁷ This mishap obliged us to travel over 300 miles on foot back to the Green River valley, the place appointed for the rendezvous the next year. We did not winter in the valley, however, but wandered about from place to place as we had done the previous winter.⁶⁸ The cold this season was very severe; at times even at midday it was very uncomfortable.

This winter's experience decided me, as also some others of our company, to seek a warmer climate, and having heard many wonderful stories of California, we settled upon coming here."⁹ In the spring, there were a large number of trappers gathered at the rendezvous in Green River valley⁷⁰ and among them Capt. Walker and Company,⁷¹ bound for California.⁷²We joined him,⁷³ making a party in all of 36. Upon the breaking up of the rendezvous we started southward, intending to trap a short time on the Marys River. The Indians troubled us so much, however, that we found it impossible to remain; they stole our traps and made it necessary to be continually on our guard to prevent an attack. They became very bold and at last offered to let us go through their country unmolested if we would give them our horses and meat. They spoke the Snake tongue, a language which most of our men were familiar with.⁷⁴ We continued to travel along and they followed us, gathering additional force, as they proceeded, from other villages. Just before we gave up trapping entirely, they shot at one of our men, by name of Frazier, while he was setting his traps, and it was only by the veriest chance that he escaped them.⁷⁵ From this time on, we doubled our guards and our precautions, making detours from the trail when necessary to avoid passing through narrow defiles, thickly wooded places and all other places favorable for an ambuscade. A few days before reaching the Sierra Nevada mountains we found that our trail passed through a large, thick body of willows, and, as we had seen the Indians around the day before, we determined to avoid the willows by making a detour in the adjoining plain. This precaution saved some lives if not those of the whole party. Hardly had the trail been left when the Indians, to the number of 400 to 500, emerged from the thicket; they formed in several distinct bodies or companies, representing no doubt the respective villages to which they belonged.

We halted and prepared for a fight. Thirty-four of the Indians advanced in a body, and 15 of our men, myself among the number, were ordered out to meet them. From 50 to 60 yds. from our company, we halted and awaited the Indians. We allowed them to get quite close before opening fire, but when we did shoot it was with such telling effect that but *one* of the 34 escaped. This appeared to completely dishearten our enemies for they permitted us to pass without further opposition.[10] After entering the mountains, I went ahead one day with the Capt. and another of our men to select a camping place with water; we became somewhat separated in our search, and upon entering the timber I discovered fresh signs of Indians. This alarmed me somewhat as I feared for the Capt. and our companion, who, like myself, had probably each taken a different course. I had just begun to look about for more signs when, glancing back in the direction I had come, I saw two Indians, with heads down and at a trot coming along my trail. I supposed that they were following my tracks, so I lost no time in getting behind a tree and preparing for them. It took them some few minutes to reach me and in the meantime they would stop every few yards and look back, and listen as if pursued. I saw that they had not seen me or discovered my tracks, as they passed within a few feet of me, jabbering as they went along. I at first had a notion to let them go but the death of my brother, so treacherously murdered by these red devils, was too fresh in my mind. The Indians were travelling in single file, and watching my chance, just before they would have to turn around a small point of rocks, I fired, shooting both of them dead at the first shot. I took their blankets, the only articles they had worth taking, as they were armed with bows, and returned to the company.[11] This was the last of the Indians. In June of 1834[78] we crossed the Sierra Nevada mountains and came down through a valley between the Merced and Tuolemi [Tuolumne] rivers,[79] into the San Joaquin Valley. Here we found an abundance of elk, deer, and bear. In Nov. following, we arrived at Gilroy's Ranch[80] and went into camp close by, where we remained about a month.[81]

While here the men employed themselves in hunting deer for the pelts. Leaving our camp at Gilroy's, we proceeded to Monterey, where we arrived about the middle of Dec. Here we spent Christmas.[82] Shortly after, Capt. Walker returned to the mountains[83] with some 20 men.[84] He was one of the best leaders I have ever met, a good hunter and trapper, thoroughly versed in Indian signs and possessed of good knowledge of the mountains. He could find water quicker than any man I ever met.

Later he returned to Cal. on his second[85] trip. I remained in Monterey with a few others of our company.[86] Here I met Yount,[87] who had been in Cal. some time. He was about to return to S[an]. F[rancisco]. and invited me to go with him and to make an otter and beaver hunt around the Bay and up the San Joaquin River. I sent my baggage in a Russian brig and I accompanied Yount in his canoe. We hunted a little on the Petaluma side of the Bay and then proceeded to the San Joaquin River, where we trapped with very fair success for about two mos. We returned with about 30 beaver, 2 sea otter, and 14 land otter. Sea otter skins were then worth $30 ea., land otter $2, and beaver about $4. While on this hunt, we found among the Tulares a little Indian girl that had been abandoned by its parents probably.

One afternoon, having found a strip of dry land among the tules, we decided to camp there for the night. As we landed, Yount saw what appeared to be Indian huts about a quarter of a mile above us on the same strip of land, and while he got supper I set out to reconnoitre. Arriving at the huts I looked into them all, but found them empty. I passed on some distance but saw no signs of Indians. It was dusk when I started on my return. In repassing the huts I heard a moan, then others in succession, which I traced to one of the huts. Looking in, I saw nothing at first, but my eyes soon becoming accustomed to the darkness I made out a small child seated in the farther corner of the hut. I went in and the little thing tried to talk to me but I could of course understand nothing of its language. I left it and returned to camp, where I found Yount somewhat alarmed at my absence, and who, when I told him of the child and proposed to go back and get it, would not listen to me. He was afraid the Indians might return in the night. All night it seemed as though I could hear the little one's cries. Early in the morning I went to the huts and found the little one so weak that she could not sit up. Upon bringing her out of the hut, we found her nothing but skin and bone. She had probably been without food for three or four days. We took her to camp and gave her a piece of boiled beaver, and it was pitiful to see the eagerness with which she caught it to her mouth and sucked at it voraciously. We feared to allow her to eat too much at first, and so took the meat from her after she had sucked it a few minutes, but so tightly did she have it pressed to her mouth that main force was necessary to take it from her. We made clothes for her and with a little care she soon recovered. When we returned from our hunt Yount took her home with him, after having her baptized and christened at the mission of San Francisco.

A few weeks after our return to S. F., Yount took a contract from Capt. A. B. Thompson[88] of Santa Barbara to furnish him with 20,000 shingles[89] for his hotel, which was then being built and is now known as the San Carlos.[90] He offered to hire me but I informed him that I was not in the habit of working for wages. I soon after took passage on the "California," Alfred Robinson,[91] supercargo, and came here to Santa Barbara. Here I met a hunter by the name of Sills,[92] an old acquaintance of the mountains, who had come to Cal. with Gant. We agreed to hunt together on the Islands.[93] At that time it was impossible for newcomers to procure a license. Capt. Denny [Dana],[94] the Capt. of this port, had a license, and Burton,[95] Sparks[96] and other hunters then here hunted under his license, paying him a share of the skins.

We had made the same arrangement with Capt. Denny and 8 or 10 days after I arrived here Sills and I went to Santa Rosa Island. We had no boats so were obliged to hunt from land. We went over about May of 1835. Two weeks later Sills was taken sick and returned to Santa Barbara. I remained about six weeks longer and killed in all 8 or 10 otter; Sills having got none. I had with me a Kanaka Indian, employed to swim out for the otter killed; at $16 a month.

I hunted under Capt. Denny's license for about a year and a half or two years. Burton and Sparks had just come from a hunt on the Islands, when Sills and I went over to Sta. Rosa.

Soon after his return Sparks went up to Monterey to see a new schooner that was being built by a Mexican, at that place. The schooner's name was to be "Peor es Nada";[97] of about 20 tons burthen. He charted her for a trip on the Lower California coast; a man by name of Charley Hubbard[98] being put in command by the owners.

Sparks was accompanied by Burton and a hunter by name of Dye.⁹⁹ They returned about Sept., I think, having made a very poor hunt owing to their failure to agree among themselves. They got, I believe, only 25 skins when they should have secured 200 at least, as the otter were plenty, the N. W. Indians not having been there for some years. The N. W. Indians did hunt along that coast afterward and killed a great many otter. In the following Oct. after the return from the Leeward, as Lower Cal. was called, Sparks went over to San Nicolas Island.¹⁰⁰ Others accompanied Sparks and among them Williams,¹⁰¹ of the Chino ranch in Los Angeles Co., and who was with me in the Mts.; he, with Col. Bean, having shown the white feather in our first engagement with the Indians, on the Ark. River. They removed the Indians, some 17 or 18 men, women and children, from this Island to San Pedro, and thence to Los Angeles and San Gabriel. I have heard from Sparks an account of the affair but do not remember the details distinctly. Some one in Los Angeles authorized the removal of these Indians, the last of the inhabitants of San Nicolas, but with what object I do not know, and cannot remember if I have ever heard. I am sure Williams had an interest in the matter, as he afterwards took one of the Indian women to live with. Having got the Indians together on the Island, they took them to the beach and put them on board the schooner. They then took them direct to San Pedro having, however, left one Indian woman on the Island. Of the exact manner in which she was left I do not now remember, but am under the impression that Sparks told me that it happened in this way. Having got all of the Indians down on the beach, one of the women wanted to go back to their *rancheria* for her child that had been left behind, which she was allowed to do. While she was absent, a strong wind sprang up and, fearing for the safety of the schooner should they wait longer, they put off from shore and ran before the wind. Arriving safely at San Pedro, the Indians were landed, from whence they proceeded to Los Angeles, where a portion of them remained; the rest being taken to San Gabriel. One of the Indians, however, a large powerful man, was left at San Pedro. He lived on the beach among the hunters, where I saw him several times. I think he was one of the most muscular men, white or Indian, I ever saw. He was but a little above the medium height, heavy set and full and broad shoulders and chest. He was partly foolish, from a fracture of the skull received in a fight with the N. W. Indians, but he was perfectly harmless and invariably good humored. He was always willing to work, cheerfully performing the most fatiguing tasks, ofttimes without being solicited. If a boat was to be hauled ashore he would frequently rush into the water, catch hold of the boat and run it high and dry on the beach, a feat that usually required from 3 to 4 ordinary men to perform. I also saw him take under his arm and bring a considerable distance to the shore a spotted seal that had been shot from shore. This seal would weigh not less than 300 to 400 lbs., besides being very awkward to handle. It would have required 3 men at least to bring it ashore. I never heard what became of him. The schooner "Peor es Nada" was ordered to report at Monterey immediately to take a cargo of timber to S. F. and thus no time was given them to return to the Island for this woman, although I think it was the intention of the same party to go back as soon as possible.[102]

The "Peor es Nada" sailed for San Francisco with timber and was capsized or foundered off the Golden Gate, her crew being saved. It was afterwards reported that, having drifted to sea, she was picked up by the Russians, but nothing definite was ever known.

Throughout the entire length of the coast it was known that an Indian woman had been left on the Island of San Nicolas, but no attempt was ever made to rescue her or to learn her fate, and as years passed on, all agreed that she must have perished. For many years after the loss of the "Peor es Nada," the only craft on the coast were small boats to which the long distance and rough sea of the outer rim of the Channel would render a trip extremely dangerous.

Eighteen years elapsed before anything further was done to ascertain her fate, when in 1853 she was found alive and brought to Santa Barbara.[103]

After my return from the Islands, I met a Negro, an otter hunter, who had been here some time, having deserted from the "Pilgrim," a trading vessel from Boston; his proper name was Allen Light[104] (he was very dark skinned) but he was always called "Black Steward." He was quite intelligent, well behaved and mannerly, and a good hunter. With him I made a hunt up the coast as far as Point Concepcion. We each had a boat and one Kanak. Made a very short trip and got 21 otter skins.

When Sparks returned from the Lower Coast, he and the Black Steward and I agreed to hunt together and were taken over to Santa Rosa by the "Peor es Nada" immediately after the Indians were taken off San Nicolas.

We remained all winter on the Islands, making our headquarters at Santa Rosa, although hunting on San Miguel and Santa Cruz, as there were very few otters on Santa Rosa. We got altogether on this hunt 60 skins.

I also made a second trip up the coast with Black Steward before going on the Islands with Sparks. We went as far up as San Luis Obispo; were gone 3 or 4 months, and got 50 otter skins. We paid Capt Denny 40% of our skins; he furnishing our provisions and paying the wages of one man for each hunter.

About the first of January 1836 we had a fight with N. W. Indians on the head of the Santa Rosa Island.

There were on the Island at the time Sparks, Black Steward, and I, hunters of our party; O'Brien[105] an Irishman, Mathers[106] an American, 3 Kanakas, and Harry Plomer[107] an Englishman, and our cook. Besides our party, there was a Portuguese called Manuel, also a hunter, and 2 Kanakas as help, making in all 12 men.

On the N. E. side of the Island and close to the present wharf there is a large cave. Its entrance is hardly larger than an ordinary doorway, but [the cave is] so large inside that a hundred persons could occupy it with ease. Here we kept our provisions and other supplies. About the first of January [1836] Sparks and some of our men saw a brig, one day, in the upper part of the Channel, and remarked casually that they were perhaps N. W. Indians. Coasting or trading vessels being frequently seen in the Channel and the N. W. Indians not having visited these parts for some time, we all took it for granted that the craft seen was a trading vessel. This appearance of the N. W. Indians would not have surprised us, as we knew they were likely to come at any time, and having talked the matter over long before, we had agreed to fight them at least as long as we could; to this the Portuguese also agreed. Sparks and Black Steward, while hunting together before, had been driven up into the Island by these Indians and their supplies captured; but we determined to defend ours as long as it could be done.

His Life and Adventures

One morning a few days after sighting the brig, we were hunting off the head of the Santa Rosa [Island]. It was very foggy, and at about 7 o'clock we started an otter and began running it towards the head of the Island.

Black Steward was about ¼ mile from shore, I was nearly opposite him and distant about 300 or 400 yds. farther out, while Sparks was between us and a little to the rear. Just as we were rounding the point the Black Steward called out, "Here come the N. W. Indians." Sure enough, just ahead of us coming out of the fog were 5 or 6 canoes pulling with might and main to cut us off from the shore. Each canoe had two Indians and some of them a third. When Black Steward called to us, the foremost canoe was but a few hundred yards away and the other only a short distance in the rear.

The fog had prevented us from discovering them, while our shooting had indicated to them our exact position. At the first alarm we made a straight line for the shore and our men needed no urging to exert themselves. We all made for a small cove or bay just below the point and lined with thick bushes. Black Steward was the first to reach the beach. Jumping out as soon as his boat grounded, he turned and fired on the foremost canoe, but the powder having partly escaped from his gun the ball fell short. A moment later Sparks reached shore and almost at the same time I jumped out on the beach beside him, amidst a shower of buckshot, the Indians having already opened fire. At that moment the first canoe was not over a hundred yards away and the others close behind. Sparks fired at the foremost canoe, wounding one of the Indians, who fell, but raised again just in time to receive my shot, which settled him. This was a reception they little expected and they turned back until a safe distance from us, exchanging shots with us in the meanwhile. As soon as each of us fired his first shot, we took refuge in the bushes, under cover of which we soon drove them out of range. We killed 3 and wounded 4 or 5 of them, while none of us received a scratch. All of our men excepting O'Brien had made for the hills as soon as we landed, not even waiting to haul the boats up, and their steps hastened by the buckshot that had already begun to whizz around us. O'Brien was given a gun but he was not a very good shot. The whole number of canoes in the attacking party was 13, each canoe having two men and many of them an extra man. In a canoe there were generally two guns but not unfrequently they carried three. In hunting otter they generally used buckshot, their arms being the old English musket, and this is the reason why they first used buckshot with us. After the first shot they loaded with ball, as they saw we were determined to make a stand. The range of these guns is something incredible. Our men assured us that the bullets from the Indians' guns passed them when they were fully a mile from the beach. The canoes having gotten out of range, they rested for a few minutes and then pulled off to the brig, which we could now plainly see about a mile away; the fog having lifted. We then left our cover, drew the boats well up on the beach and buried them in the sand, likewise our provisions, lest the Indians should return. This being done we moved back to a hollow a short distance from the shore, where we could watch the vessel without being seen, and awaited further developments. The rest of the day passed without any further movements on the part of the Indians.

At nightfall most of our men returned to our camp. We kept watch that night but saw or heard nothing. Daybreak discovered to us the brig about 2 or 3 miles away.

About 9 A.M. we saw them lower their canoes, eleven in all, and start towards shore. Arriving within a short distance they began to paddle about as if in search of otter. They continued to manoeuvre about in this manner for some time. They gradually approached the cave, passed by it, and repassed it as if without any intention of landing; finally they proceeded to a point 300 or 400 yds. below and there stopped to fish in the kelp just opposite it. Loth to lose this chance, we instructed Black Steward and O'Brien to remain and keep a lookout while we crept down to the point to get a shot at them if possible.

We reached the point unseen and were about to fire, when the men at the cave raised the cry that the Indians were landing. We ran back just in time. Just before we reached the cave Black Steward and O'Brien both fired at the two Indians in the first canoe but missed them. Our shots brought down one of them, whereupon [they] turned and put off, firing as they went. They again went off to the brig. The two days following, the brig lay becalmed, without any further attempt of the Indians to return. On the third they sailed away and we never saw them again. On the morning of the second day, as soon as the canoes started for shore our men made for the hills again but returned that same evening, and after the brig was out of sight we went back to the cave.

During all this time we had not been there lest the Indians should see us and perhaps suspect that we had our supplies there. Three days after our fight the valiant Portuguese, Manuel, came to camp half starved, having wandered about the interior of the Island without any food. At the sound of our first shots he and his Kanakas took to the hills and did not venture back until they saw the brig leave. The first day they were sure we had all been killed and the second day they were surprised to think that there were any of us left to fight. They could hear the firing distinctly, although from 2 to 3 miles away.

This defeat was a severe blow to the N. W. Indians who for several years had been the terror of the Coast. This was the first reverse they had met with. They had been in the habit of running hunters on the Islands and stealing their supplies and furs. On the mainland they landed when and wherever they liked, killing cattle and horses and occasionally the inhabitants; so I have been told. They usually came in brigs or larger vessels well armed with cannon; these same vessels being almost invariably owned or fitted out by Americans or English and manned and officered by men of the same nationalities, the Indians being employed to hunt.[108] Landing occasionally on the Islands, they attacked the almost defenseless natives, killing many of them, as the piles of human bones on these Islands, especially on that of San Nicolas, abundantly testify. Sometime before I arrived in this country, I am told, the Mexican Govt. fitted out a vessel for the purpose of guarding the Coast, preventing contraband, and especially to capture some of these N. W. otter hunters. She was lying at Santa Barbara when the "Bolivar,"[109] an American vessel engaged in otter hunting, dared him [her Capt.] to attack, running close by the Govt. vessel, her six guns shotted, and with matches burning. The Capt. of Govt. vessel acknowledged that he could do nothing, having no good fighting men among his crew. The year before I came here, Sparks told me, an American brig came down with N. W. Indians and anchored near Santa Rosa, where he and several other hunters were at the time. Some one proposed to capture her, to which all gave a willing assent. There were Sparks, Higgins, Thompson, Joaquin a Portuguese, and about 8 others who joined in the plan. Thompson[110] was to be the leader. They started off in the night, reached the brig, and were about to board her when, hearing a noise, Thompson was afraid that they were discovered and insisted upon giving it up, much to the disgust of Sparks and two or three others who did not believe in that way of doing things, but the majority were of the same opinion as the Capt. or leader, and so they returned to shore.

A year after the fight with the N. W. Indians, we ran across two of the crew of the brig, from whom we learned that she was an English ship commanded by Capt. Bancroft,[111] and that her crew was mostly foreigners.

They told us that in the first day's fight we had killed 3 and wounded 4 or 5 of their Indians and on the second day had wounded one, who received two bullets in the thigh within a $\frac{1}{4}$ of an inch of each other, which were no doubt made by Sparks and I, as we fired both at the same time and both of us good shots.

They had not used their cannon, of which they had several, because they could not see us. On the second trip of this brig, something over a year after, we learned that, owing to some trouble about rations, the Indians rose and killed the Capt. and also shot his wife, who interposed her body between her husband and his murderers. She was half Kanaka, and her death was supposed to be accidental.

Long before I came here, the N. W. Indians had hunted the otter along the whole length of the coast from Lower Cal. North, and they must have killed a very large number, as in early times they were so abundant that the Indians killed them with spears.

When I arrived here, they were still quite plenty but they were soon hunted out. In hunting, the N. W. Indians used buckshot and usually sent several canoes together so that they could almost surround an otter, thereby rendering escape almost impossible.

About the 10th or 12th of April, 1836, we started from Santa Cruz to Santa Barbara when a very strong South Easter sprang up and it was with difficulty that we made land at Goleta several miles above Sta. Barbara. During the same storm, Capt. Hinckley's[112] bark, a merchant vessel, went ashore at the mouth of the Arroyo Burro 1½ miles N. of the Light House.

A few weeks later we again fitted out, this time for a trip up the coast. When we reached Piedra Blanca, Sparks returned to Santa Barbara, bought Foxen's[113] house near the site of Crane's Hall, and opened a trading store. Black Steward and I continued up the coast, and did not return until Nov. following. We got about 60 skins. This was the last trip we made under Capt. Denny's license.

Two weeks after our return, Alvarado and his force arrived here on their way to Los Angeles.[114] I was then staying at Burton and Branch's, at the time the only boarding place in town, there being no hotel. Alvarado and Graham came to see us. Alvarado offered us $2 per day and the privilege of taking up vacant lands if we would join him. I accepted the offer. Alvarado's force consisted of about 100 men; 40 were foreigners under Graham,[115] whose Lieut. was John Cappinger,[116] an Englishman who had served in the English army; the remaining 60 were Californians. Among the foreigners whose name[s] I can now remember were, Thompson who had hunted with Sparks, two Portuguese, Manuel and Joaquin. We remained here a few days, perhaps 8 or 10, and then proceeded to San Buenaventura. Thence, after being delayed two or three days by a storm, we marched towards San Fernando. On the way we received several threatening messages from

Rocha,¹¹⁷ who commanded the Don Carlos Carrillo¹¹⁸ party at San Fernando, assuring us of his determination to destroy us if we persisted in advancing. Not in the least intimidated, we continued our march to San Fernando until within 6 miles of the Mission, where we camped for the night. We prepared for a fight the next morning, not doubting that, after so many threats, a show of resistance, at least, would be made.

The next morning we continued our march until we arrived on the plain within half a mile of the Mission. Here we halted, the foreigners dismounting and forming into line preparatory to advancing to the attack of the enemy, who, to the number of about a hundred, were already formed outside the Mission, in full view of us. As soon as our line was formed, the order was given to advance. The enemy broke and ran before we were half way to them. They were all well mounted and they did not spare their horses. The last we saw of them, fully two miles away, they were still running at full speed. We made no attempt to follow them. We took possession of the old Mission, its only inmate an old man; Don Ign[aci]o del Valle's father.¹¹⁹

After 3 nights' stay at San Fernando we proceeded to Los Angeles. Here we met several of Don Carlos Carrillo's party and among them Roach,¹²⁰ who assured us that it was his intention to fight us at San Fernando but he could not make the men stand. I am inclined to think that they did not care to face the foreigners, for whom they had a wholesome respect, especially the riflemen or hunters. A week later we left Los Angeles for Santa Barbara. Upon our arrival at this latter place, we each, Black Steward and I, received from $30 to $40, from Alvarado.

Soon after, we resumed our hunting, making a trip up

the coast as far as Monterey. On this trip we were accompanied by a man by the name of Simmonds,[121] who had learned to hunt and shoot a little having been with us on wages in one of the boats for several trips. We were about 2½ mos. in reaching Monterey and got something like 50 skins. We found a ready sale for them to a German trader by name of Myers. He paid Black Steward and Simmonds cash for their skins, but asked me to wait for my pay until I should return to Santa Barbara, which I did, and where he afterwards paid me. Simmonds no sooner received his money than he took to drinking and left us. Myers paid us $35 apiece for our skins, and, I believe, sent them to Mexico. Black Steward and I hunted back, killing about 30 otter. Several months after, Simmonds returned to Santa Barbara completely broke, having not only spent all his money but also sold his gun and boat.

This year [1837] I decided to avail myself of Alvarado's offer[122] by taking up a ranch, as for a long time I had determined to settle in the country. I had wandered over the greater portion of this part of Cal. and had seen no section that suited me better than what is now San Luis Obispo County. Having arrived at Branch's ranch,[123] whose owner had invited me to make [it] my headquarters, I started out in search of a location and immediately found the Wasner[124] ranch, which suited me very well. I hunted about a little longer, not knowing but that I might find a place that would suit me still better. I was nearly a year hunting, and searching for a ranch, during which time I spent over $500. Soon after selecting the site of the Wasner ranch, I went to see Alvarado but was put off with some excuses and so a second, third, and a fourth time, until, being pressed to give me a definite answer, he said that notwithstanding his promise it would be impossible

His Life and Adventures

for him to give me a grant of land, owing to a law recently passed by the General Govt. that only those foreigners married to Californians could take up lands. I had, in the meantime, employed Capt. Denny to make a plan of the locality, which I brought with me to Santa Barbara. Sometime afterwards, Sparks induced me to give him the plan promising to get the grant for me and, since the site was plenty large enough, we could divide it between us. He in some manner obtained the grant but never gave me an acre of it. At this time game was very plenty in San Luis Obispo Co., especially deer and grizzly bear. Of the latter I killed 45 this year [1837]. The natives hunted them occasionally but, for their mode of hunting, with the lasso, required open ground, while the grizzly seldom left the thickets and timber. Here I had several adventures with bear. My horse which I usually rode was a large, powerful one. One day while riding through a dense thicket not far from Branch's ranch, a she bear with two yearlings sprang upon us, so near that my horse barely had time to jump one side, turn, and dash out of the thicket. All this the horse did of his own accord, as I did not see the bears at that moment. I attempted to control him but found it impossible, as the bears were so close behind that I think for a moment the old one had hold of his tail. Just before the horse reached the clearing, he ran under an oak tree whose lower limbs knocked me off, one of them hitting me in the forehead and almost knocking me insensible. I laid [lay] perfectly quiet where I fell and all three of the bears rushed past me so close that I could have touched them. I lost no time in getting up a tree, knowing that they would soon return. Having followed the horse to the edge of the thicket, they turned back snuffing and grunting until they reached my tracks, which they soon followed to the tree. Looking up the tree, they discovered me and raised up on their hind legs, growling fiercely and scratching the bark off.

They soon left me and went back into the middle of the thicket. I returned to the ranch, procured another horse and some dogs, and returned. I found my horse about a half a mile from this thicket. A Mexican had come with me, so, after finding my horse, we returned to the thicket. We made the dogs go in and followed with our horses a short distance. The bears chased us out into the open ground. We repeated this until I got a good chance and killed one of the young ones. I did not dare attack the old one as my horse was almost unmanageable through fright, he having been chased and nearly caught once before by a grizzly, and besides I was still suffering from several bad bruises and cuts on my head and face. I could have shot one of them while I was in the tree, but was afraid that the others would climb after me. About two mos. [months] after this affair, I discovered the old one and remaining cub one day, eating acorns, when, creeping upon them, I shot the old one first and then the cub. I knew the old one by its having one short ear. Another day, having seen fresh tracks, I followed them down into a hollow with a thick strip of willows running through it. I had almost reached them when I saw four full grown bears. I quietly turned about and rode back. They saw me and set up a loud grunting but did not attempt to follow me; neither did I care to go after them. Mr. Branch had been chased several times by grizzlies, narrowly escaping them, so that his wife was very much exercised over my persistent hunting of them. She was continually cautioning me about exposing myself. I shot that year, as before stated, 45 grizzlies, not counting those that got away in the brush, most of them no doubt fatally wounded, but one of my rules was never to go into a thicket if I knew it contained a bear. I killed some very large ones and one in particular whose skin I sold to one of the trading vessels. It was much larger than any bullock's hide they took on board.

My mode of hunting the grizzly was this. If I discovered them feeding I rode as near as possible with my horse, keeping always to leeward; then dismounting, I tied him with a small cord which he could easily break if the bear got after him. I then approached the bear cautiously and under cover if practicable, taking advantage of the ground, timber, &c. I would get as near as 40 or 50 yds. and under no circumstances did I shoot at a longer distance than 100 yds. I never shot at the head, as unless a ball could be put fairly in the eye or ear, the constant motion of the head when feeding and its shape make the glancing off of the bullet almost certain. The breast is a good place to aim at if the bear is facing you, but I prefer the side, just back of the fore shoulder. The aim should be at a spot well back of the shoulder, as a bear's heart lies much farther back than that of a deer or buffalo. Here a shot is almost sure to drop a bear dead in his tracks; sometimes they will run a few yards, but very rarely do they move from where they are shot. One objection to shooting them in the breast is the danger of striking some of the larger bones against which the bullet flattens. On the side the ribs are the only bones and they are easily broken or even pierced by an ordinary sized bullet. If I approached them through timber, I always looked about me before firing and selected a tree that I could readily climb in case of need. When feeding, they are easily approached, by keeping to leeward, as, although their scent is extraordinary, they keep no watch; relying no doubt upon their poweress [prowess].

When a she bear with cubs is found, it is best to shoot the old one first and the young ones can be shot at leisure, as they will not leave the mother. I never shot at a bear unless I could see him plainly and was within good range, and in this way I *never* missed one. In a thicket a bear has one most decidedly at a disadvantage, and under no circumstances should they be followed, however severely wounded. If a person is cool, a good shot, and above all prudent, there is but little danger in hunting bears. Most of those I shot this year, and in fact at all times, I killed almost as easily as I could a squirrel. A person who is not a good shot, cool, and cautious, and has a good rifle, has no business to hunt bears. Nowadays with the magazine and breech-loading guns, bear hunting is very tame. In my time we had only muzzle loaders and although, by carrying two guns, we had a reserve shot, our chances were poor if a wounded bear got after us. It will sometimes happen that, in passing through bushes, one comes suddenly upon a bear and then of course his chances are poor. When a grizzly is lying in a thicket and hears a noise, it keeps perfectly quiet until the animal or person is within reach.

At this time there was no sale for bear skins, so that we never took the trouble to skin them unless for our own use or to make a present to some friend or acquaintance. Sparks killed very few bears, but he got chased by one once, and had such a narrow escape that I could never prevail upon him afterward to hunt them. In fact, he became so much afraid of them that, when we were together in a bear country, he would never leave me and often prevented me from shooting when I had a good chance at one.

Why a man who is a good shot should be afraid of a

bear under ordinary circumstances I cannot imagine, yet my experience has been that very few even among hunters care to hunt the grizzly much. There are plenty who will talk about what they would do, but they *will* run when it comes to the point. I think I must have killed, on this coast, at different times, upwards of 200 grizzlies. While at Branch's ranch I usually hunted alone, but on one trip took with me an American, a young man, green, awkward, from New England I think, who had been cast away on a whaler somewhere along the coast and was then in the employ of Branch as a laborer, or ranch hand. He was no more afraid of a grizzly than of a sucking calf; it was not courage, however, but stupidity. Having killed several deer about six miles from the ranch, and knowing they were short of meat, I decided to send my companion in with some venison.

We had made a camp from which a plain trail led to the ranch. Loading his horse with meat I started him off with the instruction to keep to the trail and to hasten forward as fast as possible in order to reach the ranch before nightfall. The next day, while out hunting I found him wandering about on foot, and completely lost. Shortly after leaving camp the day before, he found a large tree fallen across the trail and, thinking to make a short cut to the ranch, he left the trail and struck out in the direction he supposed the ranch lay. Night came on and he could see no ranch. He wandered about until the horse gave out, when he abandoned it and continued his search for the ranch on foot. So he continued to wander all that night and the next day up to the time I found him. A short distance off we found the horse quietly grazing; the meat still lashed to her. How either of them missed being caught by grizzlies, I cannot imagine. We were in the very worst grizzly country in Cal. and the horse with fresh venison would have proved a dainty morsel for them. I asked the New Englander why he did not go around the tree and continue to follow the trail. He looked a little surprised and foolish and finally said that he might have done that but at the time it had not occurred to him. Not long after this I went out to hunt one morning, leaving him alone in camp. Upon returning, I found a large grizzly walking leisurely around the camp, pausing occasionally to stand up and watch the New Englander, who was seated whittling, wholly unconscious of the presence of the bear.

Even after I had shot it and told him of its actions, he did not seem in the least alarmed. We returned to the ranch a few days after this incident, and on the way I discovered a bear and two yearling cubs in a small ravine with a willow thicket at its bottom. I fired from the top of the ravine and must have wounded the bear badly as she barely managed to crawl into the thicket. As soon as I fired I called out, "I have fixed him," at the same time pointing in the direction of the willows. My New Englander, who had, as usual, seen nothing, started to run down the ravine and before I realized what his intentions were, had nearly reached the willows. I shouted to him to come back, and he turned just as the two cubs ran out at him. A moment later, and he would have been torn to pieces. He came back laughing, perfectly unconscious of the danger he had escaped. I never took him out with me again.

About January of 1838 or before, I returned to Santa Barbara. Soon after, I made a short hunt on the Islands with Black Steward and Simmonds, in which we secured 25 or 30 skins.

In April of 1838, [I] made a hunt up the coast with Sparks and Black Steward. We returned in Sept., having been gone about 5 months. We went as far as Monterey; we got about 60 skins. The following winter I laid [lay] in Santa Barbara.

In the spring of 1839, Sparks, Hewitt,[125] an American sailor, and I started on a hunt down on [the] Lower Cal[ifornia]. coast. We had 3 canoes and a large whaleboat, schooner rigged, of about 4 tons burthen. We went as far as Redondo Island and returned in 5 mos. with 109 otter skins, which we sold at San Diego for $37.00 apiece. We arrived at Santa Barbara in Sept., remained on shore about 2 weeks, and then went on [a] short hunt over to the Islands. We returned in Nov. with about 30 skins.

Soon after, I again went up to Monterey to see Alvarado about the Wasner ranch, having been to see him before on each of our previous hunts up the coast. I was still unsuccessful. While here, I went to see Graham and Nale [Naile],[126] who were raising a company to go back across the plains to the States. They urged me strongly to join them, but when I saw the few men they had succeeded in mustering, I refused, as I saw at the first glance that they were not the kind of men to go into the Mts. with, and especially since the Indians had become so hostile. Graham and Nale came to the same conclusion later and gave it up.

At this time Alvarado told me that I could get no land until I married a Californian.

Returning to Santa Barbara, I fitted out for another hunt on the Lower Cal. coast with Sparks and Hewitt. We started in April, I think the first, of 1840. Our crew consisted of Plomer, a Dane whose name I have forgotten, Roy, an Englishman, and a Scotchman whose homely face gained for him the name of Bonito; his right name I do not now recollect. Besides these we took [on] this trip, for the first time, 4 Mission Indians. They took readily to paddling and soon became very useful. These I think were the first Mission Indians ever employed by otter hunters on this coast, and they soon superseded the Kanakas. In after years, some of the hunters began to teach a few how to shoot and that soon spoiled them as, from being very docile and willing, those who learned to use the rifle became lazy and independent, even saucy. Our armament consisted of 8 rifles and 3 shot guns. Sparks and I had, each, 3 rifles and Hewitt, 2. We went as far as Cerros Island and were gone about 6 months. On our return we touched in San Diego for supplies. We anchored a short distance out and Sparks at once went ashore to buy provisions, &c. He had hardly landed when a Mex[ican]. woman told him to look out as all Americans were being arrested and driven out of the country. This Sparks would not believe until, having proceeded up town, he was met by the *alcalde,* who informed him that he had received orders to arrest him as well as all the Americans who were with him. Sparks answered that he could carry out his orders if he wished but that, if arrested, his companions would come up and release him by force if necessary. As the *alcalde* had no force there, he did not offer to molest Sparks any further. Returning to the boat, he told us what had happened, whereupon we unanimously agreed to resist any attempt to take us. Accordingly, we carefully reloaded all our guns and kept a strict watch during the next week that we laid [lay] there. The "Alert" was in San Diego at that time and her supercargo, Alfred Robinson, confirmed to us the report that all Americans were being driven out of the country.[127] About a week after our arrival, news reached us that the vessel conveying the prisoners to San

Blas was on her way to San Diego, so we dropped down below San Diego about 20 miles to a small bay, and made a camp on shore and in a position to defend ourselves. Three days after, the vessel passed within a quarter of a mile of shore and, although they must have seen us, no attempt was made to take us.

Having taken in sufficient supplies at San Diego, and without disposing of our otter skins, we returned to the Lower Coast, going down as far as Cajalo. At San Quintín Bay we found 9 other otter hunters, 4 of them Lower Californians, Black Steward, O'Brien, a man by name of Sam and some other foreigners from Los Angeles and San Diego. There were in all 9 canoes, none of them properly equipped and but very few good otter hunters among this whole party. They were making for a point low down on the Coast that had not been hunted for some time and that, it was known, abounded in otter. We, too, were bound to this place but, not knowing the watering place where all of us must necessarily stop to fill our water barrels, we determined to keep them in sight, as we knew them to be well acquainted with the Coast. They seemed to be as determined that we should not keep in sight of them, and when we started along down the Coast together, [they] tried several times without success to leave us behind. At Cerros Island we made a slight [brief] stay which they took advantage of and pulled direct for the water. We followed close after them and passed so close to [them] that, but for a dense fog, [we] would have seen them. Neither of us saw each other, however, and we continued along down the Coast for several miles to a watering place with which [we] were acquainted and here took in a supply. We lost no time in getting under way again and by a little effort reached the hunting grounds first. Before the others arrived, we had already killed 17 otter and had their skins staked out on shore. At the sight of these, the other party were not a little chagrined, but declared they would get ahead of us yet, and so proceeded farther down the Coast until they got beyond the otter grounds entirely. We did not see them again until we returned to San Diego. We had been gone altogether 7 months and secured 173 skins. We arrived in Santa Barbara in Nov. 1840.

Here I remained this winter and on February 13 [1841] was married to Miss Sinfrosa [Sinforosa] Sanchez, my present wife.[128]

In April following, Capt. Wilson[129] and Burton fitted out a hermaphrodite brig, the property of Wilson and Scott,[130] to hunt first up the coast and then, returning, to go down on the Lower Coast. Wilson took charge of the brig and furnished the hunters with everything and took half of the skins. There were as hunters, besides myself and Burton, Breck and Hewitt. We went up to just below Monterey and returned, being gone about 2½ months. Both Wilson and Burton were very close, not half feeding our men, so that those in my boat frequently refused to work, giving as an excuse that they were hungry. This did not suit me, so I left them as soon as we got back here [Santa Barbara] from Monterey. They continued south to Cerros Island, returning to Santa Barbara in July, 1841. Upon arriving here or soon thereafter, Sparks and I made a hunt on the Islands, returning in Oct. with some 20 to 30 otter skins.

In the fall of 1840 I bought what is now known as the Burton Mound[131] property from Joseph Chapman, who had purchased it from the Mission. It had been formerly used by the Fathers to slow hides in [? to slow=to prevent the hides from curing too rapidly]. I remained on shore

SINFOROSA SANCHEZ NIDEVER

until spring of 1843. In the spring of this year Thompson (A. B.) and Jones[132] fitted out their brig "Bolivar" for a six mos. hunt to Leeward. There were six hunters, Dye, one of our original Ark. company, Dawson, an American, Sparks, Hewitt, José, a Cal. Indian, and myself. We were gone barely two months, owing to our provisions giving out. Coming back we were put on allowance and suffered not a little with hunger before we reached Santa Barbara.

After this trip I remained on shore until 1845. In April of this year, Sparks, Breck[133] and I as hunters, with a sufficient crew, made a trip to the Leeward. We were taken down in the "Bolivar" and landed on the Cerros Island, together with lumber to build a boat. We hunted around Cerros Island some and then Breck and I went over to Morro Hermoso, Sparks and two of our crew being left to build the boat. The "Bolivar" had left us and gone down to Mazatlán, where she was sold. Our new boat was to be about 4 tons burthen and was the property of Thompson and Jones, who furnished the material for building her. The boat being finished, all hands went over to Morro Hermoso. Here and among the neighboring islands we continued to hunt until our return. At Morro Hermoso we found a large school of otter, killing about 85 of them. All together we got 105 skins. We had expected to hunt some below San Diego on our return but were unable to get supplies at that port.

During the following winter we remained on shore.

In Nov. of this winter [1845], Micheltorena,[134] with a force of about 100[135] men, passed through here for Los Angeles. They tried to get Sparks, Breck, and me to join them, but we did not care to. Sutter[136] was in command of foreigners, of which there were some 30. Gant,[137] Graham, Knight[138] (their pilot), Merrit,[139] and others in the party I was acquainted with. They stayed here a few days. There were about 15 of the foreigners, who acted as an advance guard. I was acquainted with several of them, and having noticed that they were careless, I advised them to keep a sharp lookout and not take any chances.

They paid no heed to this, however, and just this side of San Buenaventura, while riding leisurely along smoking and talking they were surrounded and captured; not one of them escaping.[140]

I was told that, upon Micheltorena nearing San Buenaventura, Castro retreated to Los Angeles, while the former continued to advance until near that city. Here the two forces met, when the foreigners of the lower party, Workman,[141] Rowland,[142] & others, had a talk with the foreigners of Micheltorena's party and they came to the conclusion that they would let the Californians fight it out among themselves. As a matter of course there was no fighting, it being settled by Micheltorena leaving the country.[143]

In March, 1846, Thompson wanted us to make a trip up the coast, and fitted us out with a few supplies, telling us that we could get more at Monterey on his credit. Besides me, there was Fife[144] and a man by name of McCoy.[145] McCoy had been mate of a whaler that was cast away at Monterey. He took passage for Chile in the "Famer," Capt. Thompson's ship, and was again cast away. The "Famer," and the "Vandalia," a Boston ship, were both caught in a South Easter off Santa Barbara. The "Vandalia" barely escaped, while the "Famer" went ashore at Goleta just above Santa Barbara. Her crew were saved, but had she struck a ship's length further above, every man would have perished. The Capt. of the "Famer," Nye,[146] was ashore in Santa Barbara at the time.

Charley Brown[147] was also with us on this trip, in charge of the large boat [in which] he had made his first trip with us the year before to Cerros Island, and took [where he had taken] charge of the boat we built at that time. He was a Prussian, had been a sailor, having come here from the Sandwich Islands with Capt. Wilson, and was one of the most trustworthy and steady men we ever had with us.

Arrived at Monterey we found that we could get nothing on Thompson's credit, so we paid for our supplies and hunted up the coast as far as Fort Ross, returning in Nov. [1846] with 90 skins.

On this trip, while lying at Tomales Bay, Fife, Charley Brown, McCoy, and myself started out one day after deer; we took one of the Indians, called Blas, with us. McCoy and the Indian had remained some distance in our rear, on a ridge along which we were passing; all [were] on foot. We had left them but a short time when the Indian came running up to us saying that a bear was killing McCoy. We hastened back and found McCoy lying on the ground and very badly hurt. He was bitten in the legs and back, and had some of the cords of one of this thighs literally torn out. I dressed his wounds and wrapped them up, applying to them a wild herb whose name I have forgotten; it resembles very much our tansy. This Indian we had sent [on] to camp for the rest of the men, who soon arrived with oars, with which we formed a litter and carried him to camp. The next day we took him to Bodega. Having sent word ahead, Capt. Smith very kindly came out to meet us. We left McCoy in charge of Capt. Smith's mother-in-law, a Peruvian lady, and in less than six weeks he was able to ride a horse to San Francisco. He afterwards told us that he was walking along with the Indian when they came suddenly upon a she bear with cubs. The bear no sooner saw them than, with ears back and mouth open, she rushed for McCoy, who had barely time to fire when she was on him. The bear knocked him down and made the wounds before mentioned. His shot had not struck her, at least there were no signs of blood, for he broke his gun stock over her head when she came up, which of course only infuriated her. Her cubs began crying and she ran to them or it might have been still worse with McCoy.

The first trip Sparks, Simmonds, Black Steward and I made up the coast, Black Steward had a similar adventure with a bear. We were all out hunting and became separated. Black Steward wounded a deer and got off his horse to crawl up on it and finish it. In passing through a clump of bushes, a small she bear jumped on him, and before he could defend himself, knocked him down. He was a strong powerful man, and immediately grappled with the bear. They rolled over and over for several yards, the bear biting him very severely in several places, and tearing his coat in pieces.

Watching a favorable opportunity, he attempted to draw his knife, when the bear bit him in the forearm, tearing out some of the cords. At this moment, hearing her cubs cry, she raised up on her hind legs, when Black Steward seized his gun and shot her, breaking her back. He did not stop to finish her but made for camp. The bite in his arm was very bad, and he was scratched and bruised all over. Sparks went to the place next day and finding the bear still alive killed her. He said that for a space of over ten yards square the bushes were broken down and the ground torn up, where Black Steward had fought with the grizzly.

On this last trip [1846], when we passed Monterey the Americans had already taken it. We were just ouside when the Eng[lish]. Man-of-War entered and we could plainly hear their salutes that were fired. We stayed at Monterey two or three days for supplies.[148] Upon our return we also made a few days' stay there, and found Frémont there.

He asked me if I would join him and I promised to do so as soon as we reached Santa Barbara, and I said I thought that Sparks would join him also. Here of course we heard that the Californians had risen and retaken the Lower Country but we supposed, having heard nothing to the contrary, that everything was quiet in Santa Barbara.[149]

Arriving near the port of San Luis Obispo, we landed just above the point, and from the bluff above could plainly see the houses. There seemed to be something unusual going on so we concluded not to venture any nearer. Scott and Wilson's ship was lying in the Harbor and I at one time thought of going down to her, but I finally decided not to go near them as, from their ill feeling towards American[s], I could not expect any protection in case of need. We had hardly landed when Breck, whose ranch was close by, came down to put us on our guard against a party of Totoi Pico's[150] men that were coming out to capture us that night.

We first decided to make a fight and accordingly selected a place easily defended. We buried our skins, some 75, provisions and extra ammunition in the sand, and determined that if closely pushed we three would take one of our canoes, which was hauled up ready for use, and with our skins put off out of their reach, as we had no doubt that our skins were what they wanted most. Our large boat with the rest of our crew was some distance from shore. Fife, Charley Brown and I were on shore. All the foregoing preparations were made after supper. As soon as it got dark we proceeded to our position on a high bank overlooking and completely commanding the only approach to our camp. We drew lots as to who should stand guard the first three hours. It fell to my lot although I had hoped that I might get the first part of the night for sleeping. Fife and Brown lay down but continued to talk until I suggested that if they did not care to sleep they had better stand guard and let me lie down. They immediately got up and I lay down, but found it impossible to sleep. About midnight, having concluded that we were not likely to be attacked, I suggested that we continue our voyage. We accordingly got under way and continued down the coast the rest of that night and all the next day, the weather being too rough to allow us to hunt. Before night the weather grew worse and the wind blew fearfully. Night came on so dark that we could hardly see a boat's length. The wind, a North Wester, increased in fury until we had to run before it. We tied our boats together and some of the men tried to sleep, as all of us were nigh worn out. Since starting we had been able to cook no food and we were all wet to the skin. The sea was running mountains high, the waves breaking at least a half a mile off the shore. In the morning we rounded Point Concepcion and the change was wonderful; as south of the point the sea was quite smooth. We had decided to take advantage of the first opportunity to land and make some coffee, &c., but being anxious to arrive home we concluded to keep on since we were so near. We arrived early in the day. We had hardly landed when a party of Californians came down and arrested us and took us before the *alcalde* Anto. Ma. Ortega[151] and Raymundo Carrillo.[152] We were examined separately as to our movements, &c., during our absence from Santa Barbara. Brown and Fife were allowed to go free because they were foreigners.[153] I was retained a prisoner because I was an American. I told them that they had better leave me unmolested, but they said I must go to Los Angeles.[154] They permitted me to sleep at Sparks' house that night, he being responsible for me. The next day they made me pay $200 on my skins, an arbitrary duty, as I had already paid for my license. Capt. de la Guerra[155] was the only person in the place who had money and from him I obtained the $200, but he compelled me to leave him as security 15 otter skins. I was then allowed to go to my house and get ready to go the next morning to Los Angeles. I told them I wanted a horse and saddle but they said I had money and could buy one, and that they would give me but a few hours in which to do it. Arriving at home my wife told me that they were searching all houses for arms, that Raymundo Carrillo and Franco de la Guerra[156] had, with a party of men, visited the house but a few days before, taking a shot gun, 12 lbs. of powder and a quantity of caps, shot, and balls. I immediately hid two of my rifles and a pistol with the powder I had brought back, but I had no balls. I purposely left in sight my third rifle, not of much account. That same evening the same party surrounded the house, made a search for arms and took my rifle. They also rearrested me. I was allowed to go, however, upon promising that I would go to Los Angeles with my father-in-law, or at least as far as San Buenaventura, and then [on] alone. They gave me a passport at my request, having taken everything from me, even my pocket knife, [although] I told them I would need it on the road to protect myself. Having reached my house, I set to work to clean one of my rifles, and my pistol, and run bullets. As soon as it was dark I started off on foot up the coast to meet Frémont. The night was very dark so that I left the town without being observed. That night I reached Dos Pueblos, about 18 miles from here. Here I hid in a ravine near the road, determined to shoot the first Californian who should come in sight, and take his horse. A short distance from me was a band of horses, and early in the morning I saw a horseman coming out towards them. When he got near enough I recognized him as Vicente Ortega,[157] one of the best Californians and men in those times, and I had not the heart to shoot him, although so mad was I at the treatment I had received that I would not have hesitated if any other man had come within range. I remained there another night and the third day returned to my house along the beach.

There were three or four Californian women at my house besides my wife, and they at all times knew of my movements but they never offered to betray me, but on the contrary kept me informed of what was going on among their countrymen. I stopped at my house all night and early the next morning went over to the foothills near Montecito, about 2 or 3 miles from town, returning to my house at night. A day or two after my return from Dos Pueblos, I was told that a small party had arrived from above, escorting Thos. O. Larkin, whom they were taking a prisoner to Los Angeles.[158] Larkin had escaped from Monterey but he was retaken. I was told to keep out of the way for a day or two as, news having come from below of my non-arrival at Los Angeles, they would probably make a vigorous search for me. I remained one night in the foothills. The next day, having taken a position on the top of a rise from which I could plainly see the road, I staid there all day waiting for the party with Larkin to pass. Sometime in the forenoon a Californian by the name of Juarez was riding along a short distance from me when he caught sight of me and, having recognized me, called out for me to come to him. To his summons I made no answer and did not move from my position. He then said that if I did not come to where he was he would have to come for me. To this I paid no attention and he rode towards me. Nearby there were bushes and into these I got and waited for him. He came up to within about 30 or 40 steps, and turned about and went away. Had he approached a few steps farther he would have been a dead man. He reported having seen me to the people in town and a party of 5 or 6 men was immediately formed and came out after me. I saw them riding about but they did not come near where I was. I am inclined to think that they did not want to find me very much. There were but few of them that did not fear me. For some time after that I continued to visit my house, almost invariably sleeping there and sometimes not leaving it for several days at a time. Our house was on the top of a slight rise from which we had a clear view of everything on all sides of us for several hundred yards. There were no trees near it then. We had a small mill for grinding our wheat, the motive power being an old lame horse.

This horse had been taken a number of times by the Calif[ornian]s. but was always returned when they found it unserviceable. As soon as it grew dark I was in the habit of taking this horse and picketing him out some distance from the house, where I let him feed until late at night.

I began to get careless, and one evening, while taking him out earlier than usual, I was seen by a Calfn. [Californian] woman by the name of Vasquez, who immediately reported it to Capt. de la Guerra, who was even at that time like a king in authority here. A party of 12 men was raised, headed by Guillermo Carrillo, Raymundo

Carrillo, and Guillermo Hartnell, Jr. They came to my house about 10 o'clock at night, surrounded it and demanded to know if I was there. We were all asleep when they came but were soon awakened by the noise.

My wife answered that I was in Los Angeles. They ordered her to get a light at once and admit them.

This was done after considerable delay, during which I hid myself. In one side of the thick adobe wall there had once been a door, but which, having been closed on the outside of the wall, left a large space in which two or three persons could stand with ease. Against this and completely concealing it was a large wooden cupboard. One might have lived there for years without discovering its existence unless the cupboard should be moved. Having entered, the Californians made as they supposed a thorough search of the house and not content with having looked into every place once, they repeated it. Above the room where I had been sleeping was a loft, which they ascended to several times. Our bake ovens, one of which was in the house, received their careful attention, trunks, boxes, matrasses [mattresses] and, in short, everything was rigidly examined. The search being ended they apologized to my wife for the intrusion and withdrew. I exercised a little more caution for the next three days, at the end of which time Frémont arrived.[159] He had hardly got into camp when I went up to see him. I told him how I had been treated and he ordered a Lieut. and several men to accompany me for the purpose of searching whatever houses I suspected as containing arms, &c. As a matter of course, I led them first to the de la Guerra house. Here we found the Capt., his son, Anto. Ma., and Cesareo Lataillade,[160] standing in the porch surrounded by several members and servants of the family.

I addressed the Capt. saying that, as they had searched my house to their heart's content but a few days before, I had come to return the favor. He flushed up a little, but soon regaining his composure, he said in his pompous and authoritative way that it could not be done. This answer I communicated to the Lieut. accompanying me, who at once instructed me to say to the gentleman that if every door, box, trunk, &c., in the house were not opened immediately, they would be broken open.

The tone and manner of the officer were not to be mistaken and the Capt., not without some grumbling, ordered his son, Anto. Ma., to open everything, at the same time handing him a large bunch of keys. Lataillade made some insolent remarks which, as soon as uttered, I interpreted to the Lieut. "Tell him to shut up at once," said the officer. I did so, and Mr. Lataillade subsided. One of the soldiers was detailed to examine the contents of the trunks, &c., under the supervision of the Lieut. This soldier said he saw a large quantity of gold and silver coin in the trunks. We found no arms, ammunition or saddles, &c. The de la Guerra's never forgave me for thus humiliating them and would undoubtedly [have] had me put out of the way afterwards had they not feared me, for long after the Americans came they continued to control if not rule the native population.

I asked Sparks if he would join Frémont and he refused. He said that he was a Mexican citizen and could not do it. This answer of Sparks I conveyed to Frémont, who said nothing but looked very much displeased. Shortly after, I overheard the men discussing the subject and it was quite evident that the proposal of some of them to raze Sparks' house and confiscate his stock, among which was a fine race mare, would be adopted, and probably carried out that very night. I lost no time in apprising Sparks of their intentions and he at once went to tell Frémont that he would join him.[161]

We afterwards learned that a party of Totoi Pico's men, under an Italian cut-throat called Antonio, had visited our camp at St. Louis Obp hrb [San Luis Obispo harbor] shortly after we vacated it, as they found our fires still burning. Just before reaching our camp, they had halted and one of their men struck a light for the purpose of smoking his *cigarrete*. They supposed that we were on the lookout, saw this light and hurriedly departed, and attributed to this man's carelessness the failure of the project. Some of them frankly admitted afterwards that they intended to kill all of us and take our skins, &c. Antonio, their leader, was afterwards killed in the skirmish at Salinas when Capt. Burrows and party were cut off.

While at Monterey we were camped on a wooded point just above the town. Here we were visited by the American officers from the "Savannah" and "Congress," and the English officers from the "Collingwood." Our camp was quite an object of interest to them, especially the Eng[lish]. officers, for it was about the same as we used in the mountains. On shore, too, most of us dressed in buckskin. They shot with us at a target with our rifles, but there were no very good shots among them.[162] I talked with the Eng[lish]. officers about the American occupation of Cal[ifornia]. and they invariably expressed themselves as pleased with the change, "because," they said, "California will now be worth something."

Both Commodore Stockton and Genl. Frémont asked me very many questions about this section and each was anxious for me to accompany them. I told them that my present circumstances would not allow me to leave the men with me before reaching Santa Barbara, but promised Frémont that I would join him at that place. From our camp I very frequently went into town for supplies and also to have a talk with some of Frémont's men who were old acquaintances of mine, one of them being the brother of Alex. Sinclair. Happening in town one afternoon, I found them shooting at a target[.] The Eng[lish] and Amer[ican]. officers had been invited by Frémont to witness the shooting of some of his most skillful marksmen. From 15 to 20 of his best shots had been selected for the purpose. A target was set up at from 70 to 80 yards. A small piece of white paper about three inches square with a small bullseye [bull's-eye] in the middle was the center of the target. I was standing nearby watching the shooting, when Frémont asked if I would not like to shoot. I said that I would shoot if he wished it. A man by the name of Martin,[168] an acquaintance, and now living near Gilroy (and I understand is now blind), was there and had a fine new rifle. This he urged me to take, [I] having brought none with me. I fired three shots and put all three of my shots in the paper and close together. One of Frémont's men did the same, but the remainder of them although putting every shot very close to the paper when they did not hit it, failed to get all three within the paper.

While here in Santa Barbara, Frémont was camped just back of the "Sisters' College." He staid here about a week. The first day we moved down to Carpinteria where we remained all night. The next day we got into San Buenaventura early in the afternoon and went into camp on the South side of the river.

Shortly after we arrived, our scouts came in and reported a body of the enemy's cavalry approaching from the direction of the Santa Clara River. We immediately marched out beyond the Mission and formed. The enemy soon appeared to the number of about 80 on a low ridge but a short distance away. A field piece was run out, and two shots fired at them. At the second shot, scattered them and they were soon out of sight. Several of us wanted to follow them but Frémont would not allow us to scatter. The next day we moved up along the Sta. Clara River. Soon after starting, we saw numbers of the enemy's horsemen, ahead of us but scattered, and they continued in sight until we reached Saticoy when they crossed the river a short distance above us. During the day a Truckee Indian belonging to our party got off some distance from the column, when a few of the enemy made a dash for him, but he succeeded in getting back to the column. That night we camped just above Saticoy on the N. side of the river. The following morning we continued our march, keeping along the river, and catching an occasional glance [glimpse] of small bodies of the enemy. They kept at a considerable distance, apparently watching our movements. In the afternoon we camped at the San Francisquito ranch, on the S. side of the river. That evening, by order of Frémont, all arms were discharged, cleaned, and reloaded, as we did not know how soon the enemy might attack us. The next day we followed the San Fernando trail until we reached the foot of the mountains. Small parties of horsemen, probably reconoitring [reconnoitering] parties, appeared in our front from time to time as on the previous day. We camped at the foot of the mountain somewhere about 3 or 4 P.M. Upon our arrival, about 80 of the enemy appeared on the ridge in our front and spread themselves along its top, evidently with the object of making a show of their forces.

Here they began to throw up breastworks, and as they

had left word at San Buenaventura that we should not pass the *cuesta*, we expected to have some trouble with them here. That night the guard was doubled but nothing occurred to disturb us. The next morning about 8 o'clock 200 men were ordered to dismount and, dividing, advance up the ravines on either side to the summit of the ridge, and surround the enemy. This was executed without opposition and upon reaching the top of the *cuesta* we found the enemy gone. We took up our line of march again still following the trail. A short distance beyond the *cuesta*, a tempor[ar]y excitement was caused by the sight of men among the neighboring timber, but it was soon over when our advance found them to be Indian woodchoppers from the San Fernando Mission. We reached this Mission about noon. Here we found a foreigner with a letter from Stockton to Frémont awaiting us. Not liking his looks, Frémont ordered him to be retained as a prisoner. Commodore Stockton informed Frémont of his arrival and occupation of Los Angeles and offered to send him reinforcements if needed. We stayed at the Mission that day and the following one marched to Cahuenga, where the treaty was signed,[184] and thence to Los Angeles. Just before we arrived at Los Angeles, we were met by Andrés Pico, who gave Frémont one of his finest horses.

We remained at Los Angeles about ten days when, having been discharged, Sparks and I returned home, arriving in Santa Barbara about the last of Jan. 1847. That spring the volunteers from N[ew]. Y[ork]. arrived here and after camping near the beach for some time, removed to the Saint Charles Hotel. Soon after, two companies of them were sent South.

I remained on shore until Mar. 1848, when Sparks, McCoy, Fife and I fitted out for a trip on the coast N. of S[an].

F[rancisco]. We shipped our canoes, &c., from here to S. F. There we built a 5 ton boat which was placed in charge of Charley Brown. In May [1848] we started and hunted up as far as Cape Mendocino. Twelve miles above San Francisco we found a few otter and a few more in Drake's Bay, but above this for a long distance there are no otters. On the S. side of Cape Mendocino, we ran ashore and camped for the purpose of killing meat. The Indians, having discovered us, soon began to collect until there were from 300 to 400 camped but a short distance from us; most of them were armed with clubs and bows and arrows.

Several of them tried to approach camp, but we motioned to them to keep away and as they saw that we had our guns in our hands they went away. We built a small fort of drift wood to protect ourselves. About this time it began to blow so strong that it was almost impossible to keep one's feet. The wind continued for 3 or 4 days. During the blow the men began to get frightened about the Indians and so we decided to leave as soon as the wind stopped. It fortunately stopped at midnight and we lost no time in getting away, as we were certain that the Indians would attack as soon as the blow was over; it being impossible for them to shoot their arrows straight in a strong wind. Farther down the coast we again landed and finished getting our supply of meat.

We next landed at Fort Ross and here for the first time we heard of the gold diggings. The prospect of getting $16 a day when their monthly wages barely amounted to that was too great a temptation for our men, who insisted on leaving us at S[an]. F[rancisco]. Arrived at this latter place we sold off our skins (some 20), and paid our men. We then proceeded up the Sac[ramento]. River and allowed our men to go with us as far as they wished.

At Yuba we left our large boat and with our small boats proceeded up the Feather River. Here we separated, after dividing our supplies, of coffee, sugar, &c., that we had brought with us, and each man began working on his own account. I had brought with me from Santa Barbara a Mission Indian. He had been with me already 2 years, and he now stood by me. He was very sober and industrious. Our claim yielded us about 15 ounces a day. It was a very rich claim, however; the rest of our companions whose claims adjoined ours did not do as well. So intense was the heat that [on] the 4th day every man was down with the fever. I was the first to recover and was obliged to look after the others. As soon as possible we moved farther down the river. Here my Indian died. We then moved still farther down the river, when O'Brien died. This decided us to leave the diggings, and, besides, Sparks was still quite sick. At S. F. we took passage on a sailing vessel for Sta. Barbara, paying each $70 for our passage. The vessel was a trader and came very slowly down the coast; this enabled me to do some considerable hunting. I kept our table supplied with game, such as wild geese and ducks, &c., and in consideration of this contribution the supercargo deducted $20 from my fare.

About the last of March 1849, I again started for the mines with Davis, a Norwegian, and several natives of this place. I think there were 15 of us all together. Before reaching San Luis Obispo, we were joined on the road by a surgeon who had been under Taylor in Mexico. At San Luis Obpo. Burton joined us. We went to the San Joaquin River where we were joined by Capt. Walker and 2 or 3 men, who accompanied us as far as Stockton. From here, we went to the mines between the Tuolome [Tuolumne] and Stanislau[s] rivers. Here Burton left us. I staid in this neighborhood all summer, prospecting considerable, working many claims, but none of them rich. This section was literally alive with people. The following winter I went down near Knight's Ferry and hunted deer for about 2 months. I sold them for an average of $10 apiece, and made about $400 more than I had made the whole season at mining. Near this same Ferry I staked off a piece of land and laid the foundation for a house, intending to return soon and settle there.

I came back to Santa Barbara in Jan. 1850. So many reports reached me here of the numbers of people dying where I intended to settle, that I gave it up and never went back there. This same month [Jan. 1850], I sold my house and place to Hinchman.[105] I then went to S. F. and bought a small schooner of 17 tons burthen, with which I returned to Santa Barbara and in that [year] and in the following year of 1851 made a few short hunts for otter. In the latter part of 1850, Capt. Alden with the "Quickstep" came here to survey among the Islands. He employed me as pilot for about two weeks, paying me $10 a day.

Soon after buying my sch[ooner]. in S. F., I bought out the interest of a man by the name of Bruce who had sheep on the San Miguel Island. In Feby. following, I took 45 head of sheep and 17 head of cattle over to the Island. I had a few sheep but was obliged to buy some to make up the number, for which I paid $10 apiece. I kept this Island about 17 years. From my original stock 45 sheep, 17 cattle, 2 hogs and 7 horses I had in 1862, 6000 sheep, 200 cattle, 100 hogs and 32 horses. In the drought of 1863-4 I lost 5000 sheep, 180 cattle, a few hogs, and 30 horses.

In 1865-6, Mr. Chaffee of San Buenaventura offered me $10,000 for the Island, but finding that there was no

His Life and Adventures 77

purchaser to be found who would pay him an advance of from $2000 to $3000 on this sum he backed out. I afterward in 1870 sold it to the Mills Bros. for $10,000.[166] I had no desire to dispose of the Island, but my sons persuaded me to do so as they had become tired of living there. I have not been to the Island for several years, but I am told that [it] is almost covered with sand.

In April of 1852 I went over to the Islands[167] with my sch[oone]r. accompanied by a foreigner by name Tom Jefferies,[168] who is still living here, and 2 Indians, for sea gull's eggs. These eggs were in great demand at that time. We went direct to the San Nicolas[169] and having arrived early in the day, Jefferies, one of the Indians, and I landed and travelled along the beach towards the upper end of the Island some 6 or 7 miles. At a short distance from the beach, about 200 yds., we discovered the footprints of a human being, probably of a woman as they were quite small. They had evidently been made during the previous rainy season as they were well defined and sunk quite deep into the soil then soft, but now dry and hard. At a distance of a few hundred yds. back from the beach and about 2 miles apart, we found 3 small circular enclosures, made of sage brush. Their thin walls [were] perhaps 5 feet high, and the whole enclosure 6 feet in diameter, and with a small narrow opening on one side. We examined them carefully, but found nothing that would indicate their having been occupied for a long time as the grass was growing within them. They all occupied slight rises of ground. Outside of the huts, however, we found signs of the place having been visited not many months before. Around each hut and a short distance from it were several stakes or poles, usually from 4 to 6, some 7 or 8 feet high, which were standing upright in the ground, and pieces of seal blubber stuck on the top of each. The blubber was already dry, but I do not think it could have been there more than 3 or 4 mos. We had come on shore early in the morning and having found these signs of the existence of some person on the Island, we intended searching further, but a N. Wester sprang up about 10 A.M. so that we were obliged to hasten back to the vessel.

We had seen enough to convince us of the existence of some human being on this Island who in all probability must be the Indian woman of whom Sparks had so often spoken. The gale that had suddenly sprung [up] increased in violence until we feared it would carry us out to sea. Our anchor began dragging and we were obliged to improvise one by filling a large sack with stones. We were lying on the S. side of the Island, and were in a measure protected from the wind, but still it blew very strong even there, and the swell was very great.

The gale continued for about 8 days, at the end of which time we ran over to the Santa Barbara Island, but had no better success in finding eggs than at the San Nicolas. Here also we found several sch[oone]rs. at anchor that had come with the same object as we. We remained here but one night and then returned direct to Santa Barbara, our trip having been entirely profitless. Soon after I made a trip to Santa Cruz for lumber. The following winter I fitted out for another trip to the Sn. Nicolas Island. On our former visit I had seen plenty of otter, and besides I knew that they must be abundant as they had not been hunted for years. This time Charley Brown [Dittmann] was with me. Upon my return from my first trip I told several persons that we had seen footprints, &c., on the Island, and Father González of the Mission, having heard of it, requested me to make all possible search for her. Arriv-

His Life and Adventures

ing at the Island, Charley and I, with two Indians went ashore. We landed near the lower end of the Island and, as I and Jeffries had done, we proceeded along the beach towards the head of the Island, leaving our Indians in charge of the boat.

At the head of the Island I sat down to rest and Charley went around the point and some distance down the other side. When he returned he told me that he had seen fresh foot prints leading from the beach up to the high ridge which forms the head of the Island. He had followed them from the beach up over the high bank but beyond this they disappeared, the ground being covered with a species of moss. At one place he saw where she had apparently sat down to rest, and a small piece of drift wood lying near which had no doubt fallen from a bundle of wood she was carrying from the beach for her fire. I was at first inclined to think that our Indians had wandered off and [that] it was their footprints he had seen, but a moment's reflection showed me that it was impossible. On our way up we had also seen 7 or 8 wild dogs about [as] large [as] a coyote, and resembling one in appearance, except that they were of a black and white color. They ran away as soon as they saw us so that we could not get within range of them. I was afraid these dogs had eaten the woman as we had found nothing of her. In coming up along the beach we passed a low sandy stretch about a half mile wide that extends across the Island some distance below its head. Here we found some high bushes, called by the natives *malva real*, and in the crotch of one of these a basket made of grass and covered with a piece of seal skin. Taking it down and uncovering it we found it to contain several skins of the shag, cut square, a long sinew rope as neatly and evenly twisted as any common rope, some bone needles, &c. These

I proposed carefully replacing, but upon a second thought scattered them about and threw the basket on the ground. Charley protested against this proceeding, but he was satisfied when I explained to him that, if they were replaced in the basket by our next visit, we might be sure the woman was alive. We returned on board in the afternoon and the next day continued or [our] search without finding anything more. We then began hunting otter which we found very thick. The 3rd or 4th day, however, a South Easter sprang up and after 6 or 7 days, finding that it still continued and the sea becoming very rough, we ran over to San Miguel where we found a good harbor. Here we laid [lay] until the gale was over when we returned to Santa Barbara. We remained on shore during the rest of the winter.

In May of 1853 I fitted out my sch[oone]r. for a trip to Turtle Bay to prospect for gold. Mr. Forbush of this place had been told by Capt. Barney, an old whaler, that there was gold quartz thereabouts, and being convinced that there was something to be made, persuaded me to make the trip. Beside[s] us two there were Charley Brown, Tom Jefferies, and 4 Mission Indians. We found a very few small pieces of quartz with the least sprinkling of gold but nothing more so we gave it up, returning to Santa Barbara in July, having killed some 15 or 20 otters on our way back.

Ten days after our return I again fitted out for a thorough hunt among the Islands, and principally around the San Nicolas. Charley Brown accompanied me as hunter, and an Irishman whom we called Colorado from his florid complexion, with three Mission Indians manned our boats, while a fourth Mission Indian acted as cook. We reached the San Nicolas early in the day and at once went ashore for the purpose of selecting a camping place as we intended to make a stay of at least two or three months. We landed about the middle of the Island on the N. W. side, and went up towards the head of the Island. A high rocky bank ran along the edge of the water, its base for the most part being washed by the sea. A few short stretches of sandy beach occurred here and there but they were not always accessible from the bank. About ½ mile from the head of the Island we found a good spring of water just above the edge of the beach, and in the wet soil surrounding it more footprints that must have been made but a short time before. As it was already late and we were some 6 or 7 miles from the sch[oone]r. we were obliged to return without further search, determining however to make a thorough exploration of the Island on the following day.

Accordingly, the next morning early, as soon as we had breakfast, all hands but the cook went on shore, at the same place where we had landed the day before. Having on our previous visits seen most of the latest signs near the head of the Island, and, besides, there being but few springs in the middle and lower portion of the Island, we decided to search first from about the middle up towards the head. The four men struck across the low sandy stretch before mentioned, and found the basket and its contents carefully replaced in the crotch of the bush in which we had first discovered it. Charley and I struck up towards the head of the Island. Having become tired, I sat down to rest and Charley continued around the head of the Island. Reaching the place where he had seen the footprints the day before, he followed up the ridge. Near its top he found several huts made of whale's ribs and covered with brush, although it was so long since they had been occupied that they were open on all sides and grass was quite high within. Looking about in all directions from this point, he discovered at a distance, along the ridge, a small black object about the size of a crow which appeared to be in motion. Advancing cautiously towards it, he soon discovered it to be the Indian woman, her head and shoulders, only, visible above one of the small inclosures resembling those we had before discovered. He approached as near as he dared and then, raising his hat on his ramrod, signalled to the men who were then recrossing the low sandy stretch, and were plainly visible from this point.

They saw the signals, and came towards him. In the mean time, the old woman was busily employed in stripping the blubber from a piece of seal skin which she held across one knee, using in the operation a rude knife made from a piece of iron hoop stuck into a piece of rough wood for a handle. She kept up a continual jabbering to herself and every few moments would stop and look in the direction of our men, whom she had evidently been watching, her hand placed over her eyes to shade them from the sun.

Upon his first approach there were some dogs near, which began to growl. These the old woman sent away with a yell but without looking in the direction of Charley. The men having come up, they quietly surrounded her to prevent any attempt at escape.

This being done, Charley stepped around in front of her when, instead of showing any alarm, she smiled and bowed, chattering away to them in a language wholly unintelligible to all of them, even to the Indians. They seated themselves around her, after having made signs to me to come up. I at first did not care to go to where they were as I supposed that they had simply discovered something that excited their curiosity and I would hear about it when they should come down. They continued to make signs to me to come there, however, so I went up and found them seated around the old woman. She smiled and bowed to me also, and having taken a seat she took some roots of two different kinds, one called *corcomites* and the name of the other I do not know, and placed them in the fire which was burning within the inclosure. As soon as they were roasted she invited us all to eat some. The site of the inclosure or hut where we found her was on the N. W. side and near the top of the ridge that forms the upper end of the Island. It was not far from the best springs of water, near to the best point for fish and seal, and it commanded a good view of the greater portion of the Island. Just outside the inclosure or wind break, as I should call it, was a large pile of ashes and another of bones, showing that this had been her abode for a long time. Nearby were several stakes with blubber on them, as we had seen around the others (inclosures). There was blubber also hanging on a sinew rope, similar to the one already described, which was stretched between two stakes. Near the inclosure were several baskets, some in process of construction, also two bottle-shaped vessels for holding water; these, as well as the baskets, being woven, and of some species of grass very common on the Island. There were also several other articles, as fishhooks made of bone, and needles of the same material, lines or cords of sinews for fishing and the larger rope of sinews she no doubt used for snaring seals on the rocks where they came to sleep. The old woman was of medium height, but rather thick. She must have been about 50 yrs. old, but she was still strong and active. Her face was pleasing, as she was continually smiling. Her teeth were entire but worn to the gums, the effect, no doubt, of eating the dried seal blubber. Her head, which had evidently been for years without any protection, was covered with thick matted hair, that was once black, no doubt, but now it had become of a dull brown color. Her clothing consisted of but a single garment of the skins of the shag, made in the form of a gown. It fitted close at the neck, had no sleeves, was girded at the waist with a sinew cord, and reached nearly to the feet. She had another dress of the same material and make in one of the baskets. These were sewed with sinews, the needles used being of bone. This place was undoubtedly where she usually lived, but in the rainy season she lived in a cave nearby. Having been requested by the Fathers at the Mission of Santa Barbara, to bring her off in case we found her, I asked the Indians if they thought she could be taken by force if necessary. They thought she could. Charley Brown was of the opinion that no force would be necessary in taking her. I thereupon made signs to her to go with us but she stared at me seemingly without comprehending what was wanted. Charley then placed his hand on her shoulder to call her attention and then went through the motions of putting her things in baskets and then these on his back, at the conclusion of which he said *vamoose.* This she understood without any difficulty, for she at once began putting her things into her baskets. Her basket filled, she put it on her back and followed the Indians towards the beach while we walked behind; each of us carrying some of her things. Seal meat, some of it stinking, and a seal's head from which putrefied brains was running, was all carefully put into the basket. We soon arrived at a spring of water where we stopped and on some stakes which we found standing near we hung the things we were carrying, fixing them on the stakes in such a manner as to lead her to believe we took very great care of them. Near this spring there were several rocks, in the cracks of which were large numbers of fish and other bones, carefully placed. We then proceeded to the beach, where a spring issues from a shelving rock, just below the bank. The old woman stopped here to wash, the men having gone on ahead, and Charley and I remained on the bank above. This being finished, we proceeded to the boat and went on board the sch[oone]r. When we put her into the boat, she crept forward to the bow where she knelt, holding firmly on to either side of the boat. As soon as we got on board, she crept along side of the stove which was on deck. Dinner was ready and was at once served. The cook gave the old woman some pork and hard tack, which she seemed to relish, and in fact she took readily to all of our food, it always agreeing with her. Charley Brown at once set to work and made her a petticoat of ticking, [with] which, with [and] a man's cotton shirt and a black neck tie, he completed her dress, and she seemed to be very proud of it. Seeing Charley at work on her petticoat, she made signs that she wanted to sew. Accordingly, she was given a needle and thread, but Charley was obliged to thread it for her as her eyes seemed weak.

I had given her an old cloak or cape that was almost in ribbons and she sewed up all the rents and holes. Her manner of sewing was peculiar. Placing her work across her knee she thrust the needle through the cloth with the right hand and pulled the thread tought [taut] with the left. The next day we went ashore and camped, about the middle of the Island, close to the beach. We made a temporary shelter by spreading a sail over two oars driven into the side of the bank. A similar shelter was made for her of brush.

We remained here hunting about a month, when we brought her on shore with us. While on the Island with us, she busied herself in going for wood and water, about a quarter of a mile distance, and [in] working on her baskets. She brought water and wood of her own accord, the water in the vessels before mentioned.

Of the several baskets she was working [on], not one of them was completed, although she would work first on one, then on the other. One day Charley shot a she otter off shore. It was brought to land for the purpose of skinning [it]. Inside of her was a young otter, within a few days of being born. The carcass was being hauled down to the water, as was customary after taking off the skin, when the old woman vigorously protested against such a waste of meat. Seizing one of the flippers she drew it back on land, where it lay until the stench obliged us to throw it in the water. By this time, however, she had come to the conclusion that our food was better than this, and she so expressed herself in her own rude way by signs. She was very fond of sugar, and in fact anything sweet, and showed her fondness for it by smacking her lips. She had evidently known hunger as she sedulously saved every scrap of food and bones, and the latter she would take out from time to time, suck them over and over, and then put them away again.

When we took her from her hut, she was very careful to place the seal's head in the basket although it was almost rotten. The young otter was skinned and stuffed, making a plaything for the old woman. She hung it by a string from the roof of her shelter and for hours at a time would amuse herself like a child in making it swing back and forth, striking it with her hand to keep it in motion. One day, while out hunting, I came across her lining one of the vessels she used for holding water. She had built a fire and had several small stones about the size of a walnut heating in it. Taking one of the vessels, which was in shape and size very like a demijohn, excepting that the neck and mouth were much longer, she dropped a few pieces of asphaltum within it, and as soon as the stones were well heated they were dropped in on top of the asphaltum. They soon melted it, when, resting the bottom of the vessel on the ground, she gave it a rotary motion with both hands until its interior was completely covered with the asphaltum. These vessels hold water well, and if kept full may be placed with safety in a hot sun. When we left the Island for Santa Barbara, we were caught in such a violent gale that we were several times on the point of turning back, but we finally got under the lee of Sta. Cruz Island, which afforded us some shelter until late in the day when the wind went down. As soon as it began to blow, the old woman conveyed to us by signs her intention to stop the wind. She then knelt and prayed, facing the quarter from which the wind blowed [sic], and continued to pray at intervals during the day until the gale was over. Then she looked at us and smiled as much as to say, "You see how I have succeeded in stopping the wind." From Santa Cruz we ran over to Santa Barbara, arriving there early the next day. Upon nearing the shore an ox-cart came in sight when the old woman's delight was unbounded. She clapped her hands and danced, pointing the while at the cart and oxen. On landing I found my sons at the beach awaiting my arrival, one of them being on horseback.

Her delight at the sight of the horse was even greater than that manifested at the sight of the ox-cart. As soon as she got out of the boat, she went up to it and began examining it, pointing at this part, then that, and talking and laughing to herself. Finally she pointed at the horse and placing two fingers of her right hand astride the fore finger of her left, she imitated the motion of a horse. The news was not long in spreading, of the arrival of the old woman, and we had barely reached my house with her when half of the town came down to see her.

For months after, she and her things, as her dress, baskets, needle, &c., were visited by every body in the town and for miles around outside of it.

The old woman was always in good humor and sang and danced, to the great delight of the children and even older ones. She often visited the town and seldom returned without some present. The vessels that touched here usually brought passengers who, hearing of her, came to my house. The Capt. of the "Fremont," one of these vessels, offered to take her to San Francisco and exhibit her, giving me one half of what he could make. Capt. Trussel of this place offered me $1000 for her for the same purpose. We had all become somewhat attached to her, however, and consequently refused to listen to these proposals.

The same day [that] we arrived here, the Fathers from the Mission came down to see her. They continued to visit her, and also sent for Indians from different parts of this section, and speaking different Indian tongues, in hopes of finding some one who could converse with her. Several came, each representing a different dialect, but none of them could understand her or make themselves understood. She was continually talking and frequently made use of the *pickininy,* in referring to her child. She also used *mañana.* She expressed a great many ideas by signs, so plainly that we readily understood them. By signs she told us that she did not find her child, that she wandered about for days without tasting hardly any food or drink, sometimes sleeping but little, until her clothes were torn, and her feet and legs bleeding.

After a time she forgot her child and sang and danced. She also told that she was very sick at one time; that she had seen vessels passing two [to] and fro but none came to take her off; that she saw us on the Island before we found her.

Her dresses, bone needles and other curiosities were taken possession of by Father González, with my consent, and sent to Rome. About 5 weeks after she was brought over, she was taken sick from eating too much fruit and 7 weeks from the day of her arrival died. The Fathers of the Mission baptised her *sub conditione* and named her Juana María.[170] I left here for San Francisco just before she died, having first made her a rough coffin. My wife can tell you better about her after I brought her ashore.

Since this date I have remained here in Santa Barbara making an occasional otter hunt.

The foregoing sketch of my life was dictated by me to Mr. E. F. Murray, and having been carefully read to me I find it correct.

(Signed) GEORGE NIDEVER

[A facsimile of the concluding page of the manuscript will be found on page 90.]

FACSIMILE OF A PAGE OF THE MANUSCRIPT

NOTES

[1] A writer in the *Santa Cruz Sentinel*, June 14, 1873, names John Nidever as among those who came to California with the Walker party in 1834 [1833], but Bancroft thinks that he came later. Captain George Nidever, Jr., the only child of the subject of this narrative still living (1935), feels certain that his uncle John came to California in 1851 or 1852.

[2] *Infra*, 16.

[3] Nidever evidently had a confused recollection concerning "Crawford" County and the "Moro" River. At the time Nidever left Missouri in 1820 or 1821, there was no Crawford County. This county was organized in 1829. It was created out of Gasconade, an original county. Moreau Creek runs across Cole County, which is also an original county, about three miles from Jefferson City, and empties into the Missouri six miles below. Because of Nidever's evident confusion, we are unable to determine whether he lived on Moreau Creek in Cole County, or in what became Crawford County.

[4] By a treaty made with the Osage Indians in 1808, they ceded away all their lands east of a line running due south from Fort Clark, near Kansas City, Missouri, to the Arkansas River, the whole comprising the present States of Missouri and Arkansas north of the Arkansas River to within thirty or forty miles of their western boundary. The territory remaining to them comprised the entire present State of Oklahoma north of the Canadian and Arkansas rivers, together with a small border of western Arkansas and Missouri. Nidever and his party evidently encountered the Osage Indians in this narrow range of territory, probably in the neighborhood of the Vermillion River, which flows across the northeast corner of the present State of Oklahoma.

[5] This river was referred to by hunters as Six Bull, or Six Bulls. It is now called Neosho, or Grand River. On its left bank near its mouth is Fort Gibson, which was not in existence in 1820–21. For identification of the Six Bull River, see Jacob Fowler, *Journal . . . 1821-22*, edited by Elliott Coues (New York, 1898), 3, and footnote. Nidever is correct in referring to the region where they were as Arkansas, for at the time, the Territory of Arkansas, which had been created in 1819, extended forty miles farther west than does the present State of Arkansas.

[6] When the Cherokees in their restricted territory east of the Mississippi indicated a willingness to move west, they were given lands between the Arkansas and White rivers as two boundaries, with an eastern boundary line from near the town of Morrilton in Conway County running northeastwardly to the site of Batesville. The Indians understood that the western boundary began at Fort Smith on the Arkansas and ran parallel with the eastern line to the White River. This western line, as finally surveyed in 1825, ran from Table Rock Bluff above Fort Smith to the mouth of the Little North Fork of the White River.

[7] Fort Smith was on the south bank of the Arkansas River near the western boundary of the present Arkansas, at the mouth of the Poteau

River. It was established in 1817 and named in honor of Brigadier-General Thomas A. Smith. Though situated in Arkansas, it played an important part in the affairs of the Indian Territory. It is not far south of the region of the Six Bull River, where Nidever and the party he was with stayed for two or three months.

[8] The Choctaws, like the Cherokees, had recently ceded lands east of the Mississippi for a section in the Indian Territory and a large part of western Arkansas south of the Arkansas River and south of Fort Smith. By another treaty in 1825, they ceded to the United States the land east of a line extending from Fort Smith due south to the Red River.

[9] Soon after Stephen F. Austin was recognized by the Mexican authorities as his father's successor, with permission to colonize in Texas, he returned to Louisiana and published the particulars of his plan of land distribution. Many conditions relating to settlement in the grant were still unsettled, however, when Nidever visited there.

The permission to colonize in Texas was given to Moses Austin shortly before his death in 1821, but it was not until March 7, 1827, that the demarcation limits of the grant were settled. They were as follows:

"Commencing on the west bank of the river San Jacinto, at the termination of the ten league reserve [the national colonization law provided against colonization "within ten leagues of the coasts, without previous approbation of the general executive power"], from the gulf of Mexico and thence following up the right bank of said river to its head, thence due north, to the road leading from Bexar to Nacogdoches; thence following said road westwardly, to a point from whence a line due south will strike the La Baca to within ten leagues of the Gulf of Mexico, and thence eastwardly along the said ten league line parallel with the coast, to the place of beginning."—Joseph M. White, *A New Collection of Laws, Charters, and Local Ordinances of the Governments of Great Britain, France, and Spain, Relating to the Concessions of Land in Their Respective Countries; together with the Laws of Mexico and Texas on the Same Subject,* I (Philadelphia, 1839), 613.

[10] Among the names of the original "Three Hundred" colonists of Austin's Grant, as shown by the original records in the General Office at Austin, Texas, is that of Moses Shipman. Presumably he was the father of Daniel Shipman. For the list of names see D. W. C. Baker, *A Texas Scrap Book* (A. S. Barnes Company, New York, Chicago, and New Orleans, 1875), 557–61.

[11] Alex. Sinclair and Nidever were companions from this time until Sinclair was killed at the battle of Pierre's Hole in 1832. See *infra,* 14, 27. Both of them were members of the trapping party which went out from Fort Smith in 1830. After the cowardice shown by Colonel Bean, the captain of the hunting party, Sinclair was looked up to as their leader, a position he held until he was killed.

[12] Colonel Bean proposed the forming of the hunting and trapping expedition, although he was inexperienced in such activities. He was made captain of the company because of his good name and the esteem in which he was held. But the company soon lost confidence in his bravery because

of his cowardly actions in an encounter with Indians. He was hardly treated civilly after he showed the white feather, and the company were glad to see him leave to return to Arkansas after they had reached New Mexico. See *infra*, 19.

[13] For a description of the character and location of the region known as the "Cross Timbers," as he found it in 1832, see Washington Irving, *A Tour of the Prairies* (London, 1835), 3-4.

[14] The records do not give the names of all the members of this trapping party, but most of them are known. Colonel Robert Bean headed the expedition. He was accompanied by his son, William, a quiet, sensible young man. Father and son left the company upon its arrival at Arroyo Seco, New Mexico, and returned to Arkansas, arriving there on November 1, 1831. See *infra*, 19, and the *Arkansas Gazette*, November 2, 1831. Nidever's brother Mark and a man named Crist were killed by Indians soon after the company entered the mountains.—*Infra*, 16. An old man, Judge Saunders, or Sanders, who started with the others, either died or was killed in the first year.—*Arkansas Gazette*, November 2, 1831. Alex. Sinclair and a younger brother made two more. Alex. Sinclair was killed in the battle of Pierre's Hole in 1832.—*Infra*, 27. There were several others of the company about whom a little more is known than just the names. There was Isaac Graham, who came to California in 1833, and became famous or, maybe, notorious. Job F. Dye came to California with Ewing Young in 1833, and left a valuable historical document on his experiences.—Bancroft, *California*, II, 787. A man named Price was one of those who left the Walker expedition in California with Nidever. There were with the company, also, Pleasant Austin, Powell Weaver, James Bacey, James Wilkinson, Cambridge Green, another Green, James Anderson (who was killed by Cambridge Green), and Dr. James Craig, and a man by the name of Hace, who seem to have attached themselves to Ewing Young. Others, of whom little else is known than their names, were Van Buren, Potter, Frazier, Williams, Baldwin, Allen, Bowen, Carmichael, Pollum, Nale, and a Tom Hammonds.—*Arkansas Gazette*, November 2, 1831; and Bancroft, *California*, III, 387-88, and footnote.

[15] Nidever's reference to the country through which they were passing as country "frequented by the Comanches" is one of the many evidences of Nidever's remarkable ability to recognize different Indian tribes and to remember their location.

The Comanches were one of the southern tribes of the Shoshonean stock, and the only one living entirely on the plains. In 1719 they were mentioned, under their Siouan name of Padouca, as living in what is now western Kansas. From that time on they roamed over the country about the heads of the Arkansas, Red, and Trinity rivers, in Colorado, Kansas, Oklahoma, and Texas. They made their first treaty with the Government in 1835. See F. W. Hodge, *Handbook of American Indians North of Mexico*, Part I (Washington, 1907), 327.

[16] They traveled north or northwest to the Arkansas River. They doubtless reached the river in the southwestern part of what is now Kansas, and not far from the present boundary between Kansas and Colorado.

[17] If the Indians met with on the Arkansas in southwestern Kansas or southeastern Colorado were Pawnees, they must have been wandering at the time, for this was not Pawnee country.

At some time in the past, the Pawnees established themselves in the valley of the Platte River, Nebraska. Their villages lay between the Niobrara River on the north and Prairie Dog Creek on the south. Their country was bounded on the west by the country of the Cheyennes and the Arapahoes, and on the east by that of the Omahas on the north of the Platte, and by lands of the Oto and Kansa tribes south of the Platte. This would place them in northwest Kansas, southwest Nebraska, and possibly in a small part of eastern Colorado, where they overlapped in the territory of the Algonquin family. See Hodge, *op. cit.*, Part 2 (Washington, 1910), 213–15.

[18] See mention on p. 46, fn. 115.

[19] Colonel Bean went back over the old trail of the traders to St. Louis. This is indicated in the following item from the *Arkansas Gazette*, November 2, 1831: "*News from the trappers.* Van Buren; Colonel Robert Bean got home yesterday. All the company are still trapping except three, Nideavor, Christ, and Judge Sanders, . . . Colonel Bean came by way of St. Louis and is going back shortly." The reference here to Nideavor (Nidever—Mark no doubt is meant) and Christ (Crist) is clear (see account of their death at hands of Indians, *infra*, 16), but concerning "Judge Sanders" we have no information. Nidever refers to "Saunders, an old man," as being one of the original party.

[20] He was killed at the battle fought at Pierre's Hole, *infra*, 27, and footnote.

[21] See *supra*, 14, fn. 19.

[22] Arroyo Seco was between five and ten miles from the Rio Grande, on the Arroyo Hondo, which flows into the Rio Grande about forty miles from the northern boundary line of New Mexico. As Nidever offers no hint of the route followed in crossing the divide between the Arkansas and the Rio Grande, I see no point in hazarding a guess concerning it. Whether he was far enough east to go over the old Taos route from the Cimarron River to Taos, or was far enough west to strike the trail from Pueblo south, or whether he passed over one of several other easy passes, there is no way of knowing.

[23] The San Fernando referred to is of course San Fernando de Taos, usually known as Taos.

[24] See *supra*, 6–7, fn. 14.

[25] See fn. 19.

[26] See *infra*, fn. 31.

[27] Ewing Young made his first journey to California from New Mexico in 1830, with a company of beaver hunters of various nationalities. In a communication to another pioneer, named Cooper, he indicated his purpose to return the next year.—Vallejo, *Documentos* (MS in Bancroft Library), XXX, 135.

The expedition referred to by Nidever was Young's second one to California. He left San Fernando (Taos) in September, 1831. He trapped along

Notes   95

the Gila and other streams on the way, arriving in Los Angeles in April, 1832.

Job F. Dye mentions, as going with Young's company, Pleasant Austin, Powell Weaver, James Bacey [Basey], and James Wilkinson. Nidever mentions these, also, and adds the names of Hace, the two Greens, and Anderson.

[28] James Anderson.

[29] Cambridge Green.

[30] The murder of James Anderson by Cambridge Green in Arizona and his delivery to the authorities in Los Angeles is mentioned, also, by Job F. Dye, in his *Recollections* (MS in Bancroft Library). Dye was with Young's party, and Nidever may have learned the story from him when he and Dye met in California in later years. Bancroft says that Green escaped from prison some time later. See Bancroft, *ibid.*, III, 388, and footnote.

[31] James Craig, referred to by Nidever as Dr. Craig, went into Sonora from San Fernando, according to Nidever, but Dye, in his *Recollections*, speaks of Craig's having crossed the mountains with him. Bancroft says there was a party from New Mexico in 1832–33 about which practically nothing is known, and he intimates that Dr. Craig may have come to California with this.—Bancroft, *loc. cit.*

[32] For additional information concerning Workman and Rowland, see fnn. 141, 142.

[33] The Indians known as the Crows were a Siouan tribe forming part of the Hidatsa group, who, according to their tradition, about 1776 went as a band from the Missouri River to the vicinity of the Rocky Mountains. Here they continued to rove over a wide area until gathered on reservations. They spent many years in conflict with surrounding Indians.

These Indians were found by Lewis and Clark on the Bighorn River. In 1817, Brown located them on the Yellowstone River, and on the east side of the Rocky Mountains. In 1834, Drake found them on the south branch of the Yellowstone, in Latitude 46°, Longitude 105°. A writer later (1862) wrote: "The country usually inhabited by the Crows is in and near the Rocky mts., along the sources of Powder, Wind, and Bighorn rs., on the s. side of the Yellowstone, as far as Laramie fork on the Platte r. They are also found on the w. and n. side of that river, as far as the source of the Musselshell and as low down as the mouth of the Yellowstone." See Hodge, *op. cit.*, Part 1, 367–68.

It is quite possible that a few wandering Crows may have been south of the Arkansas River as Nidever passed through that country, but his reference to the Snake Indians also, makes one feel as if he may have been confused in his recollection at this point either with respect to the country he was thinking of, or to the Indians encountered, or to both.

[34] If it is difficult to explain the reference to Crow Indians in the region between Arroyo Seco and the Arkansas, it is quite impossible to explain the presence of Snake Indians there.

The name Snake was applied to many different bodies of Shoshonean Indians, but most persistently to those of eastern Oregon. See Hodge, *op. cit.*, Part 2, 606. They were found inhabiting southeastern Oregon, Idaho, western Montana, and the northern parts of Utah and Nevada. They were subdivided into many small tribes.—Bancroft, *Native Races,* I (San Francisco, 1875), 422–23.

[35] The Kiowas at one time resided about the upper Yellowstone and Missouri. They were better known as centering about the upper Arkansas and Canadian in Colorado and Oklahoma. It seems that, at some time, they moved southward from the extreme head of the Missouri, driven by the Cheyennes and Arapahoes, with whom they made peace, however, about 1840. When they reached the Arkansas, they were opposed by the Comanches, who claimed the south country. First there was war between them, then an alliance. The Kiowas were noted for their predatory and bloodthirsty character.—Hodge, *op. cit.,* Part 1, 699.

[36] The size of the valley described by Nidever would correspond roughly to that of the famous Brown's Hole of the trappers at the boundary of the present Colorado and Utah, and just south of the southern Wyoming line. But as this valley runs east and west, it seems likely that Nidever refers to the rendezvous valley fifty miles from the western boundary of Wyoming, a little south of the center of the State from north to south, and about seventy miles from Jackson's Hole, which is about fifty miles south of Yellowstone Park. This valley ran north and south and had the productivity described by Nidever as characteristic of the place of their winter quarters.

This rendezvous valley is no doubt the upper valley of the Green River under the Wind River Mountains. The annual gathering here of the trappers and traders of the rival fur companies for rest and revelry in the summer months while they awaited the arrival of their winter supplies is well described by H. M. Chittenden in *The American Fur Trade of the Far West.*

[37] The headwaters of the Columbia River are in western Montana and some distance northwest of the place where the party had wintered. The "other companies" to which Nidever makes reference were of the Rocky Mountain Fur Company, the American Fur Company, and the Hudson's Bay Company. For an account of the various companies operating in the region near Pierre's Hole, and north of it, see H. M. Chittenden, *The American Fur Trade of the Far West* (New York, 1902), I, 247–48. On the particular point, see 299.

[38] The party which went toward the Platte rejoined the others at Pierre's Hole. See *infra,* 25.

[39] Pierre's Hole, as it was known then, or Teton Basin, its present name, is at the eastern edge of Idaho, its extreme southeastern end touching the western boundary of Wyoming ninety miles from its northern boundary. The Teton, or Pierre, River drains the west slope of the Teton Mountains. It rises in Teton Pass, and flows into Henry's Fork of the Snake River. The name, Pierre's Hole, was attached to the part of the valley lying along the northerly course of the river. The valley extends in a direction from southeast to northwest. It is some thirty miles long and from five to fifteen in breadth. Several trails led into this valley, and it was a resort for the trader and trapper.

Notes 97

⁴⁰ The hunters and trappers already present were the vanguard of the Rocky Mountain Fur Company's trapping parties, some free trappers, and some parties of the American Fur Company led by Vandenburgh and Drips.

William Sublette, who arrived July 6, was bringing supplies for the Rocky Mountain Fur Company, which had been organized in 1830 by a group headed by Thomas Fitzpatrick, Milton G. Sublette, Henry Fraeb, Jean-Baptiste Gervais, and James Bridges. The numerous roving bands of this company were to meet at the Pierre's Hole rendezvous in 1832, and it was quite important that their supplies should reach there before Fontenelle should arrive with supplies for the newly formed American Fur Company. Sublette succeeded in arriving first. For further light on and confirmation of Nidever's statement, see John D. Wyeth, *Oregon, or a Short History of a Long Journey* (Cambridge, 1833), *in* Thwaites, *Early Western Travels* (Cleveland, 1905), XXI, 68; Chittenden, *op. cit.*, I, 657–58; Washington Irving, *Adventures of Captain Bonneville* (New York, 1868), 69–73.

⁴¹ Fitzpatrick had set out to meet William Sublette, who was on his way from St. Louis with supplies, in order to hasten his progress so that agents of the American Fur Company, whom Fitzpatrick had met, might not capture the trade at Pierre's Hole by getting their supplies there first. He met Sublette on the Platte near the mouth of the Laramie, where Gantt, Blackwell, and their company joined the party of Sublette.

When the joint party arrived at the Sweetwater, Fitzpatrick went on ahead alone to carry the news of Sublette's approach to the rendezvous. He came upon a party of Blackfeet and, in a series of thrilling experiences, lost his two horses, his ammunition, and his weapons. When nearly used up, he met two hunters, who helped him to the rendezvous. Captain Bonneville says they were Iroquois hunters; Zenas Leonard indicates that he was one of those who found him; and Joseph Meek says two hunters found and helped him. Nidever was probably correct in the number, but he may have been mistaken in the name of the other one. See Irving, *op. cit.*, 68–73; Chittenden, *op. cit.*, I, 296–97; W. F. Wagner, ed., *Narrative of the Adventures of Zenas Leonard* (Clearfield, Pa., 1839), edited and republished by W. F. Wagner (Cleveland, 1904), 93–109; Mrs. Frances Fuller Victor, *River of the West* (Hartford, Conn., and Toledo, Ohio, 1870), 109–10.

⁴² No census was taken at this rendezvous. Although Nidever says there were 500 in all, doubtless meaning whites, there can be no certainty of the actual number present.

⁴³ William Sublette's company is variously estimated. Chittenden (*op. cit.*, II, 658) says: "He had there about two hundred trappers, or beaver hunters; or more properly speaking, *skinners* of entrapped animals; or peltry-hunters, for they chased but few of the captured beasts."

⁴⁴ Milton Sublette was an able leader, but he was less distinguished than his brother. When the Rocky Mountain Fur Company was organized, he was one of its heads. He was at Pierre's Hole in 1832 in connection with the business of his company. See Chittenden, *op. cit.*, I, 254, 292;

II, 658. Irving (*op. cit.*, 68) says: "This Captain Milton Sublet had about twenty men under his command, all trappers."

[45] Henry Frapp, as pronounced and spelled by his contemporaries, but Henry Fraeb, as signed by himself, was a member of the firm of the Rocky Mountain Fur Company from 1830 to 1834. The company referred to as his by Nidever may have been the combined group of Milton Sublette and himself under the command of Sublette.

[46] Nidever is remembering here the number of Wyeth's men who went with him after the camp broke up.—Wyeth, *op. cit.*, 31–70; cf. William H. Ellison, "From Pierre's Hole to Monterey," *Pacific Historical Review*, I, 85.

[47] Though Nidever states that five hundred persons were present, he accounts for only a part of these in his enumeration. Besides the groups referred to by him, a large number of men belonging to the American Fur Company were present under Vandenburgh and Drips. The remnants of Blackwell and Gant's parties that came in with William Sublette were present. There were in addition "many hundreds of Indians, mostly of the Flathead and Nez Perce tribes." See Irving, *op. cit.*, 72; Chittenden, *op. cit.*, II, 657–58. Wyeth, *op. cit.*, 63, says that there were about five hundred Indians. Both the Flathead and Nez Perce tribes were friendly with the whites. These tribes with the Snake made common cause against the Blackfeet.

[48] When the party under Sinclair came out of the Green River valley in March, 1832, they followed the river toward its head until May, when a disagreement arose over where they should go. So they separated, some going one way and some another, but the greater number toward the Platte. But, as we see here, they were united again at Pierre's Hole.

[49] The party of which Nidever was a member, and other parties at the rendezvous, were what were called "free trappers." These were men who worked on their own account, being bound to no company. See Chittenden, *op. cit.*, I, 3, 55, 297. Chittenden refers to Alex. Sinclair as a "partisan."—*Ibid.*, I, 298; II, 661. Captain Bonneville (quoted by Irving) gives an interesting description of the free trapper.—Irving, *op. cit.*, 85.

[50] As soon as William Sublette arrived on July 6 with the supplies for the Rocky Mountain Fur Company, business moved rapidly and was nearly completed by July 17. On this date, and not at the beginning of August, as Nidever states, nor on August 25, as Leonard says in his *Narrative* (Wagner, *op. cit.*, 111), the hunters began to leave for their respective hunting grounds.—Chittenden, *op. cit.*, I, 297–98; II, 658; Wyeth, *op. cit.*, 69; Irving, *op. cit.*, 73.

[51] The river referred to was discovered by Ogden in 1825 and named after the temporary wife of one of Ogden's men. The wife named Marie was soon dropped, as was the name given the river. The name Ogden was then given to the river, but this was changed by Frémont to Humboldt, and this name the river still bears.

[52] Milton Sublette and Captain Wyeth had set out to go to the Salmon River for the winter. This river, which is entirely in Idaho, is one of the longest and most important branches of the Snake. Its sources are in the

Notes 99

central part of the state, nearly one hundred and fifty miles west of Pierre's Hole. The river flows north, then directly west, and makes a long northward sweep before losing itself in the Snake. Wyeth's destination eventually was the mouth of the Columbia River, but he had decided to trap for a short while before going on.—Wyeth, *op. cit.*, 69 and footnote; Chittenden, *op. cit.*, I, 298; II, 658.

[63] An important fact about the Grosventres, the division of the Blackfeet encountered here, that has interest in this connection was their tribal affinity with the Arapahoes and their feeling of friendship for them. The Grosventres, Cheyennes, and Arapahoes once lived together near the headwaters of the Mississippi and in the region of the Great Lakes. Migration took place later. The Cheyennes went to the south, the Arapahoes to the southwest, and the Grosventres to the west. It was the custom for the Grosventres to visit their friends, the Arapahoes, every two or three years. Sometimes on their visit they went by the headwaters of the Snake and Green rivers and the mountains of northern Colorado in order to avoid the Crows. The encounter of the trappers with them at this time at Pierre's Hole occurred in connection with one of their return trips from the Arapahoes. See Chittenden, *op. cit.*, II, 713-23, 850-55, for an elaborate statement about them. Irving, *op. cit.*, 65-67, has some striking comments about these natives. See also Hodge, *op. cit.*, I, 508.

[64] It seems that, when at first a long line of people appeared pouring down a mountain defile, they were supposed to be Fontenelle and his party, who had been daily expected, until Wyeth observing with a field glass recognized them as Indians. Nidever's statement of their number is probably too high, and only a small part of them were on horseback. See Irving, *op. cit.*, 73.

Much to the surprise of the trappers, the Indians displayed a British flag. It was later learned that the Blackfeet captured this in an encounter with a party of the Northwest Fur Company, who had been almost annihilated by the Indians. The Indians took the flag to use it for the purpose of deceiving their enemies. See Zenas Leonard, *Narrative of the Adventures of Zenas Leonard* (Clearfield, Pa., 1839), 2-22.

[65] An element of white treachery was displayed in this event which, while explainable, is not a justifiable exemplification of rude justice in the mountains, even though the Blackfeet were hostile to the whites and to the Flathead tribes. There were friendly Flathead Indians with the trappers. One of these rode out with Antoine Godin (Nidever's Goddar) to meet the chief of the Blackfeet. The two men deceived the chief into thinking they were seeking a friendly conference. When they were near enough to fire a deadly shot, as Nidever says, or near enough to proffer a hand of friendship, as Wyeth and Irving say, one of them shot the chief dead, and Antoine galloped back to the men with the scarlet robe as a trophy. See Wyeth, *op. cit.*, 70; Irving, *op. cit.*, 73-74.

[66] Nidever rather oddly mentions only that Sinclair was shot in the thigh, saying nothing about his death, and never mentioning him again. But in an earlier part of Nidever's narrative (*supra*, 14) he says that, after the breakup of the original company in New Mexico, "Sinclair was by

tacit agreement looked up to as our leader and continued in command until he was killed."

Irving (*op. cit.*, 76–77) states definitely that Sinclair was killed by a shot through the body as he and his brother pushed into or through the edge of the wood. His statement is confirmed by Chittenden (*op. cit.*, II, 660–61), who says that Sinclair was killed on the spot as he became exposed to the fire of the Blackfeet.

[57] Only the more seasoned trappers and some Indians took part in the engagement. Wyeth's men remained in a protected camp spot by order of Wyeth, but he and some Indians accompanying him took part in the fray. The number who pushed their way through the tangled copses in the attack on the Indian fort is uncertain. Nidever says there were not many more than one hundred men, but there may have been even fewer. They were about equally divided between Indians and whites. The attack was led by William Sublette, who was injured, Robert Campbell, and Alex. Sinclair, who was killed.

[58] In the conversation between the allied Indians and the besieged Blackfeet, the statement of Nidever does not agree in details with the testimony of others present. It appears probable that the Blackfeet said that six or eight hundred of their own warriors would soon arrive, when they would give the whites all the fighting they wanted. In the interpretation of the conversation, it was understood that this big force was attacking the rendezvous camp. Following this, a large force of Sublette's men hastened back to camp. The Indians abandoned the fort in the night.

[59] In the battle, the whites lost five killed and six wounded. The allied Indians lost seven killed and six wounded. Of the number of Blackfeet killed there is no certain knowledge. Chittenden concludes that nine dead warriors were left in the fort, together with twenty-five dead horses and nearly all the Indians' baggage. Irving says that the Blackfeet admitted a loss of twenty-six warriors. Leonard says that five whites, eight Flatheads, and ten Nez Perce Indians were killed in the first encounter, and gives the total number lost in the battle as thirty-two, principally Indians. Nidever's numbers certainly are overstated, and there is no way to be certain of the casualties on the Blackfoot side. Cf. Irving, *op. cit.*, 73–80; William Sublette's letter to Ashley, in the *Missouri Republican*, October 16, 1832; Wyeth, *op. cit.*, 69–72; Chittenden, *op. cit.*, II, 658–64; Leonard, *Narrative, op. cit.*, 22–24; Victor, *op. cit.*, 111–18.

[60] After the battle of Pierre's Hole, Milton Sublette's brigade, the remnant of Wyeth's band, and the free trappers with whom Nidever and Zenas Leonard were associated, remained some days at the rendezvous to see if the main body of the Blackfeet intended to return for an attack. When they did not, the combined party proceeded toward the southwest.—Irving, *op. cit.*, 80.

[61] The Snake Indians had their habitat in the upper Green and Snake river valleys. They were not openly hostile to the whites, but they were treacherous, suspicious, and a nuisance because of their thieving and begging habits.

[62] In moving about, the party went along the southeastern edge of pres-

Notes

ent Idaho into western and southwestern Wyoming, northeastern Utah, and northwestern Colorado. From the Snake Indian region, they took a southerly direction to the Bear River, which flows into Great Salt Lake. They followed this river for a few days and then crossed over to Weber's River, which reaches the lake not far from the mouth of the Bear. From the lake, they went toward the headwaters of the Colorado. About the middle of November, they found a satisfactory valley on one of the main feeders of this river, where they halted and made preparations to spend the winter. See Leonard, *Narrative, op. cit.*, 25-26.

[63] This was the Colorado River. Trappers called it "Rio Colorado," or "Red River."

[64] The Crow Indians belonged to the Hidatsa substock of the Siouan family. The distinction made by modern writers between Crow proper and mountain Crow did not obtain among the trappers.

The home of the Crows was the valley and watershed of the Bighorn River. It may be said to have included, to the east, the valleys of the Rosebud, Tongue, and Powder rivers, and a strip of territory on the north bank of the Yellowstone. But when the "Crow country" was mentioned, the valley of the Bighorn was meant. However, the Crows were a wandering people, and they were encountered in almost every part of the trans-Mississippi region.

The Crows were finely formed physically, and they were great horsemen. Also, they were considered the most skilled horse stealers and robbers among the Missouri tribes. For this reason, and not because of hostility, they were very troublesome to western traders. See Chittenden, *op. cit.*, II, 855-57.

[65] Nidever's narrative is very unsatisfactory at this point. He has passed over several months of time in a few paragraphs in which almost no information is given. He is in error in at least one particular, for some of their stolen horses were recovered. See Leonard, *Narrative, op. cit.*, 26-28.

The expression "into the waters" means near or along a stream and its branches, or even in any part of the river's drainage area. It was frequently used by frontiersmen in this sense.

[66] Nidever speaks of "Rees" Indians, and Leonard referred to the same Indians as "Rickarees." The natives referred to by each name were the Aricaras, one of the principal divisions of the Caddoan family. They appear to have migrated north from the Red River and the Natchitoches, settling on the waters of the Kansas and Platte rivers. At one time they were more numerous than when found by the traders, this fact being indicated by the remains of villages over a wide area.

"These Indians had good physiques, being tall and well formed. Their women were considered the handsomest on the Missouri. They were a warlike people, who were on terms of hostility with most of the tribes around them. Towards the whites, they were treacherous and warlike: friends one day, enemies the next. Following Colonel Leavenworth's campaign against them in 1832, they moved to the neighborhood of the Mandans, but they soon returned, and a few years later migrated to the North Platte."—Chittenden, *op. cit.*, II, 558-607, 861-62.

[67] Nidever continues to be confused and forgetful in his narrative here. Gillum's (Gillam's) death occurred in the spring of 1832. Having seen no Indians for several days while on the upper Platte, the band of fifteen men turned their horses loose to graze. The next morning several men went to get them. Both Gillam and Leonard were along. Leonard separated from the others. He ran afoul of an Indian, and was attacked, but escaped. The others encountered more Indians. Gillam was killed, two other men were wounded, and most of the horses were taken by the Indians. See Leonard, *Narrative, op. cit.*, 30–31.

[68] Nidever appears to be thinking of two successive winter wanderings at this time when in reality there was only one.

[69] There can be little doubt that what Nidever here says about deciding to come to California was the man's thought in 1878 and not in the spring of 1833.

[70] There were present in the valley at the head of the Green River, the American Fur Company's band; the trappers of the Rocky Mountain Fur Company; Nathaniel Wyeth, then on his way back home; a party of sportsmen under an English officer, Captain Stuart; Robert Campbell with a party and outfit from St. Louis; and numerous free trappers, in all about three hundred white men.—Chittenden, *op. cit.*, 300.

[71] Nidever's "Capt. Walker and Company" is Leonard's Captain "Bowville and Company," or Bonneville. Benjamin Louis Eulalie de Bonneville, a graduate of West Point and an officer in the west, made a well-known effort to secure wealth and scientific position in a fur-trading and trapping enterprise, 1832–35. His enterprise was a failure, but he became of great service by falling into the hands of Washington Irving. Irving built around Bonneville a description of Rocky Mountain life during the best days of the fur trade.

Captain Walker was Joseph Reddeford Walker, who at this time had command of one of Bonneville's bands. Walker began his career as a guide on the frontier in 1822. In that capacity he accompanied Bonneville into the Rocky Mountains in 1832. In 1833, he conducted the party of which Nidever was a member past Great Salt Lake and across the Sierra into California. On the trip across, he discovered Yosemite Valley, and he requested that the epitaph on his tombstone should record the fact of the discovery of this wonderland. He made other discoveries on this trip. As one who guided Frémont on one of his expeditions, he became bitter in later life when the title, "the Pathfinder," was applied to Frémont, who merely followed the tracks made by Walker and his associates. See Bancroft, *California*, V, 765–66; Wagner, *op. cit.*, 146–47.

[72] There is no way of knowing the exact purpose of Bonneville in sending the party out under Captain Walker. Irving gives the date of the departure of the expedition as July 24, and he says: "The brigade set out from the Green River valley to explore the Great Salt Lake," and that, after facing difficulties in the region of the lake, "they then struck directly westward, across the great chain of California mountains . . . at length they made their way through them and came down upon the plains of New California. . . ."—Irving, *op. cit.*, 326–30.

Notes

It is difficult to understand why this expedition was supplied for a year if the Great Salt Lake were its objective, since the remotest point of Great Salt Lake, as Bonneville knew, was only two hundred miles from the rendezvous, and Bonneville himself could easily have gone there in the several years he was in the region. Irving's statement of the purpose of the expedition is not convincing. But Nidever's simple statement that the expedition was bound for California, and Leonard's statement that he hired out with the expedition as clerk because he was anxious to go to the Pacific, are evidence that California was the intended destination.

[73] Most of the fourteen free trappers in the band Nidever was with, when they were rested, hired themselves out variously with Bonneville's company. The large company was divided into three divisions, and that under Walker was to start through an unknown country, probably for the Pacific. It was to this division that Leonard and Nidever were attached.

[74] The Indians referred to were the Paiute or Digger Indians, who belonged to the Shoshonean stock. They were a degraded and pitiable people, dwelling in the desolate waste to the west and south of Great Salt Lake. They were inferior in stature, and nearly always in a condition bordering on starvation. They subsisted in large part on ants, other insects, and vermin, and also upon roots, on which account they were called Root Diggers, or simply Diggers. They had no horses, and were armed only with bow and arrow. They were usually friendly to the whites, perhaps through fear. They were harmless through incapacity to do much harm; but they were annoying through their disposition to theft.

[75] Whether it was the same person is not clear, but one morning a trapper, discovering that his traps had been stolen in the night, swore he would kill the first Indian he should meet. As he returned with some comrade to camp, he saw two defenseless Diggers seated on a river bank fishing. He crept up on them, shot one on the spot, and threw his bleeding body into the stream. The other Indian escaped with his life. He was mildly rebuked by the leader of the party for his cold-blooded murder; but that was all. See Irving, *op. cit.*, 328.

[76] These Indians were unquestionably annoying and perhaps threatening. Walker no doubt felt that there was danger of the Indians' surrounding his company. He may have said, as Jo Meek reported: "We must kill a lot of them boys. It will never do to let that crowd get into camp." Leonard says that when Walker gave orders to chastise the Indians, thirty-two of Walker's men mounted choice steeds and charged on the Indians. He gives 39 Indians killed as against Nidever's 33; Irving gives 25; Stephen H. L. Meek says 27 in one attack and 13 in another; and Joseph Meek alleged there were 75. The rest of the Indians fled. The cruel blow is approved by Nidever, defended by Leonard, and criticized severely by both Bancroft and Irving.

[77] The companions of Nidever on this occasion were Captain Walker and Zenas Leonard. After Walker and Leonard became separated from Nidever, two Indians made their appearance, but as soon as they saw the two white men they ran in Nidever's direction. If Nidever was sorry for what he did, as Leonard alleges, it is not apparent from Nidever's story.

[78] It was not in June, 1834, but in October, 1833, that the party crossed the Sierra. They began the ascent of the Sierra on October 10 or 11. They were descending to the plains on October 31, and they were still in the plains and not yet in the San Francisco Bay region on November 12, when a great meteoric storm occurred.—Wagner, *op. cit.*, 169, 180, 187. It has been established that, on November 12, 1833, there was such a meteoric shower as the one described by Leonard. See Wagner, *op. cit*, 187, footnote.

[79] Irving's account, *op. cit.*, 130, describes the passes and defiles as having the wildest scenery, sublime rather than beautiful, and abounding with frightful precipices, but he does not give much clue to the route across the mountains. Mrs. Victor's idea, which came to her from Joseph Meek, is that the party went westward to Pyramid Lake, followed a stream which they called Trucker's River, and explored across the mountain by almost the route later fixed upon for the Union Pacific Railroad.—Victor, *op. cit.*, 147-49.

Leonard's description of the approach to the mountains, of precipices more than a mile high, of dashing waters, and of big trees makes it appear quite clear that Leonard described a route across in the region of Yosemite Valley and the Merced River. See Wagner, *op. cit.*, 166-95. Stephen Meek confirms this as the route followed. Nidever's brief statement appears to be just about conclusive on the point. Walker himself thought he saw Mono Lake and Yosemite Valley. The inscription on Walker's tombstone, "Camped at Yosemite Nov. 13, 1833," was put there at his request. The date, of course, would not be quite correct. According to an article in the *San Jose Pioneer*, September 1, 1877, based on an interview, Walker's first attempt to descend the mountains was near the headwaters of the Tuolumne, which was an impossibility, but he then worked a little to the southwest and struck the Merced.

[80] It is not known by what route the trappers came to the Santa Clara Valley, but they must have traveled around the east side of San Francisco Bay to its lowest point [that is, the southern end; perhaps the present Alviso]. They then crossed the valley to the coast, where they sighted a vessel. Being signaled by them, the vessel came to shore. It was an American ship, the "Lagoda," Captain Bradshaw. Both the sailors and the trappers were surprised at this chance meeting. The trappers were wined and dined on the ship, and were told the distance to San Francisco and to Monterey. When they returned to the Santa Clara Valley, they stopped at Gilroy's rancho. See Wagner, *op. cit.*, 190-95.

"Gilroy's Ranch" was occupied by John Gilroy, the first foreigner to settle permanently in the Mexican province of California. He was baptized and naturalized in California and married into the Ortega family. The rancho on which he lived was part of the San Isidro rancho, which had been granted to Ortega. Gilroy showed the Walker party every courtesy and directed them toward Monterey.

[81] It is unlikely that they remained a month at Gilroy's, for they undoubtedly camped for a time near San Juan.

[82] There is almost nothing in the archives about the trip to Monterey, or the life of the men while there. That there may have been some fear

connected with the coming of these foreigners is possible, but certainly they were allowed freedom and were shown hospitality.—Victor, *op. cit.*, 149-52.

It would appear, according to Wagner, who, however, is not always reliable, that Captain Walker went to Monterey from San Juan in the early part of December. He was shown courtesy by the governor and leading people. Captain Bradford acted as interpreter for him. Permission was given Walker to remain in the country for a time if he would refrain from trapping on the Indian lands or trading with the natives.— Wagner, *op. cit.*, 204-05.

The company went to Monterey between December 18 and December 25. On December 29, they were entertained on board the "Lagoda." They remained in Monterey and at a mission or place referred to as St. Joseph (possibly Carmel) until February 14.—*Ibid.*, 210-25.

[83] Their route from Monterey into the San Joaquin Valley is uncertain. Once in the valley, they skirted the Sierra to the headwaters of the Kern River. With Indian guides, they found a pass and crossed the mountains near Owens Lake by what has since been known as Walker's Pass. They rejoined Captain Bonneville on the Bear River on July 12, 1834.—Wagner, *op. cit.*, 226-43; Chittenden, *op. cit.*, I, 418-21; Bancroft, *California*, III, 301.

[84] Nidever is certainly in error with respect to the number of men accompanying Walker on his return. The original company had more than 20 men. Leonard's figures are more nearly correct. According to him, there were 52 men, 315 horses, 47 beeves, and 30 dogs, together with a quantity of supplies, which they had obtained from the Californians.

[85] He returned with the Chiles-Walker party in 1843.

[86] There is no certainty of the number of men who remained in California. George Nidever and John Price are the only two names definitely known. George W. Frazer and François Moz, a Canadian, were probably two of the others. A writer in the *Santa Cruz Sentinel*, June 14, 1873, names John Nidever, John Hoarde, Thos. Bond, Daily, Capt. Merritt, Wm. Ware, and François Lajeunesse as having come into California when George Nidever came. There is no confirmation of these names, and the writer is in error with respect to John Nidever. He came about 1852, according to his nephew, George Nidever, Jr., who is still living (1935) and is certain of this date.

[87] George C. Yount went to Santa Fe in 1825, and there joined a party of beaver hunters. Part of the time he hunted with Ewing Young and James O. Pattie. He came into California with the party of William Wolfskill in 1831. Captain Dana of Santa Barbara sent for him, and Yount at once embarked upon the enterprise of sea-otter hunting under Dana. At a later date, he went to Monterey, where Nidever met him. He had a notable history in California, until his death at his Caymus rancho in 1865. See Charles L. Camp, "The Chronicles of George C. Yount," *California Historical Society Quarterly*, II, 3-66.

[88] Alphaeus B. Thompson was a native of Brunswick, Maine. He may have arrived in California the first time as early as 1825. Between 1825 and 1829 or 1830, he was supercargo of the schooner "Washington." It is said

that the first raising of the United States flag in California was at San Diego in 1829 in celebration of the arrival of that schooner with Captain Thompson from the Sandwich Islands. Between 1831 and 1834, and from time to time up to 1838, he was supercargo of vessels. After 1834, he considered Santa Barbara his home. Here he engaged in business as merchant and shipbuilder for many years. In 1834, he married Francesca, daughter of Carlos Carrillo. She died in 1841. On her death, he and their children became part owners of Santa Rosa Island, which Carlos Carrillo had conveyed to his daughters, after receiving it as a gift from the Mexican Government. Thompson died in Los Angeles in 1869 at the age of 74.—Bancroft, *California*, V, 746; Yda Addis Storke, *A Memorial and Biographical History of the Counties of Santa Barbara, San Luis Obispo, and Ventura, California* (Chicago, 1871), 36.

[89] Yount introduced shingle roofing into California. He explained the process of making shingles to the Mexican general, M. G. Vallejo, and made the shingles and shingled the house of Vallejo, the first shingled house in all the two Californias. He received in return two leagues of land.—Nellie Vandegrift Sanchez, *Spanish Arcadia* (San Francisco, 1929), 92.

[90] The San Carlos Hotel was on the south side of State Street just west of de la Guerra Street.

[91] Alfred Robinson came to California from Boston in 1829. He became the resident agent of Bryant and Sturgis, and in this capacity traveled from port to port, exchanging the cargoes of the Boston ships for hides. He married the daughter of Captain José de la Guerra y Noriega. He resided continuously on the coast for twelve years. His interesting narrative, *Life in California*, published in New York in 1846, is a valuable contribution on the life and history of the period it covers.

[92] Daniel Sill, a native of Connecticut, and a mountain trapper, came to California from New Mexico in the winter of 1832-33. He settled in Santa Barbara, where, like many others, he hunted otter under Captain Dana's (the name is given as Denny by Nidever) license. For a while he was partner in a bakery in Santa Barbara. For some years, from 1839 or earlier, he lived in San Francisco. He is named as one of the foreigners arrested in connection with the Graham affair in 1840. From 1844 until his death in 1862, he spent most of his time in the Sacramento Valley.

[93] The reference is to the Santa Barbara Channel Islands—Anacapa, Santa Cruz, Santa Rosa, and San Miguel—which lie in a line running east to west parallel with the coast, and separated from the mainland by a channel sixty miles long and from twenty to thirty miles wide. San Nicolas Island, which is seventy miles from Santa Barbara almost directly south, should be included.

[94] The reference is undoubtedly to Wm. Goodwin Dana, a native of Boston, who, as master of the brig "Waverly," came to California from Hawaii in 1826. He quickly fell in love with Josefa Carrillo, daughter of Don Carlos, but he had to wait for baptism and naturalization before the marriage could be consummated. He was baptized in 1827, obtained provisional papers of naturalization in 1828, and was married to Doña Josefa, aged 16, in the same year. Twenty-one children were born to this

union. In the course of time, he engaged in trade, agriculture, and stock raising. In 1829, the schooner "Santa Barbara" was built at Santa Barbara for Dana and Carlos Carrillo. It was to be used in trade and for otter hunting, and was licensed by Governor Echeandía in that year. Dana was given his final naturalization papers in 1835. In that same year, he was made appraiser for La Purísima Mission. He was probably captain of the Santa Barbara port, as Nidever says. He was made *alcalde* of Santa Barbara in 1836. One source of his revenue in these years was the letting out of his otter-hunting license to foreigners, who could get no such paper, they paying him a percentage of their catch. He was granted the Nipomo rancho in the region round San Luis Obispo in 1837, and he lived there from about 1839. He was a very influential man in the country round about Santa Barbara.

[95] Lewis T. Burton was a native of Tennessee. He came to California with the Wolfskill party in 1831. He settled in Santa Barbara, where he engaged in otter hunting, trade, and finally, farming. He married María Antonia, a daughter of Carlos Carrillo, and acquired some wealth from his trade and his rancho. His name is perpetuated in Santa Barbara in "Burton Mound," a slight elevation of ground at the beach, which was the site of the Potter Hotel. This mound was excavated in 1923 by the Thea Hye expedition, for the study of the extensive Indian remains lying a few feet underground. The property was purchased by Burton from A. F. Hinchman in 1860, and here he made his home until his death in 1879, when the property came into the possession of the Seaside Hotel Association. For information on "Burton Mound," see J. P. Harrington, *Exploration of the Burton Mound at Santa Barbara, California* (Washington, 1928), 31–33, 58–60.

[96] Isaac Sparks arrived in Los Angeles in April, 1832, with Ewing Young's second expedition. Soon after his arrival, he went to Santa Barbara, where he at once engaged in otter hunting. He is known particularly for three things: as an otter hunter, as the man who in 1834 removed the Indians from San Nicolas Island in the ship "Peor es Nada," and as the builder of the first brick house in Santa Barbara. This house was later known as the Park Hotel.

[97] The "Peor es Nada" was a Mexican schooner of twenty tons, built at Monterey by Joaquin Gomez, and launched August 30, 1834. Under the command of Charles Hubbard it sailed for the south in October, under charter to Isaac V. Sparks and others for otter hunting. It returned in March under John Coffin, and made a second trip in the autumn.

[98] Charles Hubbard was a German and a naturalized Mexican. He came to California in the early thirties. Besides the fact that he was master of the "Peor es Nada" in 1834–35, little is known about him.

[99] Job Francis Dye was a Kentuckian trapper. He was a member of the Arkansas party to which Nidever was attached. He left that party in New Mexico, where he joined Ewing Young's expedition to California in 1832. Late in 1833, he took charge of Captain Cooper's livestock on the Rancho del Sur. For several years this name appears on Larkin's books, and for a long time he continued his otter hunts. He engaged in business, farming,

and stock raising in various parts of California. His *Recollections of California* . . . , dictated for Bancroft in 1877 and now in the Bancroft Library, and his narrative published in the *Santa Cruz Sentinel* in 1869, contain some valuable historical data. On Larkin, see p. 66, fn. 158, *infra*.

[100] San Nicolas Island (see fn. 93, *supra*) is the most distant of the Santa Barbara Channel Islands. It is dry and sterile, although, sixty and more years ago, sheep were herded on it. It is about one hundred feet high, abrupt like San Clemente, and comparatively flat topped. It is eight miles long, with an average width of three and one-half miles. The shore line measures twenty-two miles.—Geo. C. Davidson, *United States Coast and Geodetic Survey* (Washington, 1863), 21.

[101] Isaac Williams, a native of New York, was one of Young's trappers who accompanied him into California from New Mexico in 1832. He settled at Los Angeles and engaged in trading and trapping for a number of years. He was generally known in California as Julian Williams, often signing his name in that way. He was naturalized in 1834. About this time, he married María de Jesús, daughter of Antonio Lugo. He became the owner of the Chino ranch, granted to Lugo in 1841, and was himself the grantee of an addition to the rancho in 1843. He died in 1856.

[102] Some additional information on the removal of these Indians is contained in an article published in *Scribner's Monthly* for September, 1880, written by Mrs. Emma Hardacre. She learned her story from persons who had been participants in the event, and from others who had received their information from these. Her version is the same as Nidever's in most particulars, but it is marred to some degree for historical purposes because of her effort to make it a good literary story. See Emma C. Hardacre, "Eighteen Years Alone," *Scribner's Monthly*, XX (September, 1880).

The causes of the disappearance or the methods of the removal of the many Indians who once inhabited the Santa Barbara Channel Islands may continue to be a matter of conjecture, for there is no evidence to show certainly how or when the islands ceased to be inhabited. David Banks Rogers, Curator of Anthropology of the Santa Barbara Museum of Natural History, accounts for their disappearance by natural causes growing out of contact with a different civilization, and removal of some of them to the mainland by the padres. Father Engelhardt, historian of the Franciscan Missions, stated in his writings and in private conversation that there was no documentary evidence to show their removal in large numbers to the mainland, and that he did not find any record of the removal from San Nicolas Island of the band referred to in the Nidever narrative. It seems probable, however, that the Indians removed by Sparks were the last Indian residents of the islands, except for the lone woman saved by Nidever.

[103] See *infra*, 77-89.

[104] There is little information concerning Allen B. Light other than that Nidever gives. He deserted from some vessel, probably the "Pilgrim." An account of an adventure he had with a grizzly bear is told by Alfred Robinson. He was one of Graham's men in 1836-38. In 1839, being a naturalized resident of Santa Barbara, he was appointed by the government to

prevent illegal otter hunting. He was in Los Angeles in 1841, and at San Diego in 1846-48, and at the latter time he was still a hunter.

[105] John O'Brien landed at Santa Barbara from a whaler in 1835. He was at that time twenty-five years of age. For several years he hunted otter on the Islands. In 1840, he was in the employ of Lewis Burton, and in the same year he obtained permission to marry. He was one of the first to go to the mines after the discovery of gold in 1848. He fell ill at the mines and died at Benicia in October, 1848, while being brought down the Sacramento River.

[106] Mathers was Matthews, an American. Nothing is known about him except that he hunted with Nidever.

[107] Henry Plummer was an English cooper, who landed in Santa Barbara from a whaler in 1835. He was thirty-five years of age at the time. Like so many others, he at once became an otter hunter, and he went with Nidever on a number of expeditions.

[108] It has frequently been charged that Russians used the Northwest Indians in hunting sea otter on the coast and in such marauding expeditions about the Santa Barbara Channel Islands as are here spoken of by Nidever. Captain F. W. Beechey, in his *Narrative of a Voyage to the Pacific and Bering's Strait* (Philadelphia, 1832), 331–32, makes statements which are probably the basis for most of the written charges. His allegations were denied, however, by Baron Wrangell of the Russian American Fur Company, and by Governor Figueroa, both of whom allege that other nations had committed the crimes alleged, but that Russians had not. See Dimitry Zavalishin, *Russian Affairs*, V, *The Affairs of the Ross Colony* (Moscow, 1866; manuscript translation by Mr. Klinhofstrom, in Bancroft Library), 3–5. Nidever speaks of extensive activities where Northwest Indians were employed by ship captains, but he says these were nearly always American or British ships, and neither here nor elsewhere does he implicate the Russians.

[109] The "Bolivar," an American brig, which was variously stated as of 193, 212, and 224 tons, arrived from Honolulu and valued at $7000, appeared on the coast with goods almost every year from 1832 to 1840. A. B. Thompson was supercargo of the vessel part of the time. In 1836, John C. Jones, American consul to the Sandwich Islands, made his trip aboard this brig. It was several times accused of smuggling by the Mexican Government.

[110] Presumably Captain A. B. Thompson.

[111] It appears that Captain John Bancroft, commanding the ship "Llama," was on the California coast on several occasions hunting sea otter in violation of Mexican law. Bancroft thinks the "Llama" may have been the ship whose Indians attacked Nidever and his men. It seems probable that this vessel made a successful trip in the spring of 1838, for in the summer it touched at Honolulu on the way from California to the Columbia River. The ship had on board twenty-seven northwestern Indians. The wife of Captain Bancroft accompanied him. In the autumn of 1838, with the same crew or a new one of twenty-five Kaiganies, he came down the coast and began work again, in defiance of Mexican law, on Santa Rosa Island. In November, Bancroft had trouble with one of his hunters and,

while he was standing at the gangway looking over the side of the vessel, he received mortal wounds from a volley of musket balls in the back. His wife threw herself upon his body, and she was badly wounded by a second volley of shots from the Indians. A seaman who attempted to come to their rescue was killed. The Indians seized the vessel and forced Robinson, the mate, to sail north. When the Kaiganies reached their homes, they landed with their canoes and all they could carry, and allowed the "Llama" to go on its way. It arrived at Honolulu in January, 1839, where Mrs. Bancroft died from the effects of her wounds.—Bancroft, *California*, IV, 90–91.

[112] Probably Wm. Sturgis Hinckley, a native of Massachusetts, who came to California in 1830. He was a trader at Honolulu, master or supercargo of several different vessels, smuggler, an aid to the cause of Alvarado, and an official in San Francisco. He died at the age of thirty-nine years, thus escaping arrest at the hands of Frémont's men as a Mexican official. The place where his vessel was wrecked was evidently what is now known as Hendry's Beach.

[113] This was Benjamin Foxen, an English sailor, who came to California in 1826. He was baptized as Wm. Domingo, though often called Julian. He was naturalized in 1837, married Edwarda Osuna (or Olivera), and after selling his store in Santa Barbara became owner of Tinoquaic rancho, where he spent the rest of his life. He is remembered because Frémont camped on his rancho and, it is said, was directed by him to cross to Santa Barbara by San Marcos Pass so as to avoid being attacked by the Mexicans, who had prepared an ambuscade in the narrow passage at Gaviota, where they planned to roll rocks down from the cliffs.

[114] Mariano Chico arrived from Mexico in May, 1836. He at once announced the new Mexican centralist constitution, replacing the federalist document of 1824. When he was driven out and had sailed from Monterey for Mexico on July 21, Gutierrez returned to office, accepting at the same time the centralist idea which the hated Chico had advocated.

A quarrel soon developed between Gutierrez and Juan Bautista Alvarado. Alvarado led a revolution in opposition to the centralist constitution and in favor of greater autonomy in California affairs. He soon had a company of seventy-five, who were reënforced by a mixed company of Mexicans, Indians, and Americans under Isaac Graham. Gutierrez was sent out of the country, and the *Diputación* declared the independence of the province until Mexico should return to the federalist constitution of 1824. Since Los Angeles, which had been made the capital in 1835, did not favor independence, Alvarado decided on a quick march south. Nidever joined the company when it passed through Santa Barbara, and was with it when the company entered Los Angeles on January 23, 1837.

[115] This was Isaac Graham, one of the original company of trappers with Nidever. The date of his arrival in California is uncertain, but it was probably 1834 or 1835. Although Nidever praised his bravery and loyalty, he had the worst of reputations in New Mexico and on the plains, where he was well known by B. D. Wilson, Job Dye, and others. His career in California did not improve his reputation. According to Bancroft, he

was loud-mouthed, unprincipled, profligate, and reckless; but he possessed personal bravery, was prodigal in hospitality to his class, and was a skillful hunter.

On his arrival in California, Graham gave up his legitimate trade as a trapper and hunter for the more profitable occupation of running a whiskey distillery at Natividad in the Pájaro Valley. Here he gathered about him a band of rough men with reputations as "dead shots" and "bad men." These he took with him when he joined Alvarado.

[116] This was John Coppinger, who was probably a deserter from a British vessel at San Francisco. He was said to have been a lieutenant in the British army or navy, but, according to his naturalization papers, he was American. He served as a lieutenant of Graham's forces in the years 1836–1838.

[117] The person referred to was Juan José Roca, who probably came from San Blas in 1825 as one of the company with Echeandía. He was put in command of the Monterey detachment of the San Blas company and is often named in the records of succeeding years, being *comisionado* for the secularization of San Juan Capistrano in 1833–34, in charge of San Gabriel in 1836–37, and acting commander of the southern force in the sectional war of 1837.

[118] The revolution of 1836–37 was in large measure a conflict for leadership between Alvarado and the Carrillos. José Antonio Carrillo was the provincial deputy in the Mexican Congress who had procured an act making Los Angeles the capital of the province. When Alvarado made himself governor in 1836 with Monterey as the capital, and changed the *Diputación* to the "Constituent Congress," the opposition in the south to Alvarado and independence was led by Don Carlos Carrillo.

[119] This was Antonio del Valle, a Mexican lieutenant, who came from San Blas to Monterey in 1819 with a detachment of troops to oppose Bouchard and other enemies of Spain. He served in a number of capacities after Mexican independence. In 1834–35, he was *comisionado* for the secularization of the San Fernando mission, and served as majordomo later. He opposed Alvarado and supported the Carrillos.

[120] Same as Rocha or Roca. See *supra*, fn. 117.

[121] Stephen Simmonds, a native of New York, is listed by Bancroft as one of the sixteen arrivals for the year. He landed at Santa Barbara from the whaler, "Liverpool Packet." He was an otter hunter with Nidever for several years. His name appears at Santa Barbara and Monterey in 1839–40. It is supposed that he died at Branch's rancho about 1845.

[122] *Supra*, 46.

[123] The ranch referred to here as Branch's ranch was the old Santa Manuela rancho near San Luis Obispo. Francis Ziba Branch, a native of New York, came into California from New Mexico with the Wolfskill party in 1831. After hunting a few years, he opened a store and boarding house in Santa Barbara. Occasionally he engaged in hunting again. He married Manuela Carlon in 1835. In 1837, he sold his store, and upon his naturalization in 1839, was granted the Santa Manuela rancho, and spent the remainder of his life there. He died in 1872.

[124] The ranch referred to was undoubtedly the Huasna or Huasma rancho, which was granted to Isaac Sparks in 1843, and for which his claim was confirmed by the United States Land Commissioners.

[125] George Hewitt was a newcomer, having arrived in 1839, or just before the trip to which Nidever here refers.

[126] Henry Naile was an American trapper who came into California in 1836 by way of New Mexico. He went north soon after his arrival and joined Isaac Graham at the latter's distillery. His name appears in Larkin's accounts and other Monterey records from 1838 on. In 1839, he and Graham undertook to raise a party to cross the mountains eastward, but the plan failed, as Nidever has stated, because of the unpromising material in men. For a few years, Naile was interested with Graham in a sawmill in the Santa Cruz region. He was naturalized in 1844, and was killed by one James Williams, in 1846, in a quarrel over a contract in connection with the mill.

[127] In late March or early April, 1840, Alvarado was warned of an intended uprising of Americans and other foreigners in California. Isaac Graham was alleged to be the chief of the conspirators. After discussion of the dangers of an uprising in a meeting of the *junta* on April 4, Alvarado ordered a wholesale arrest of foreigners, except such as were married to native women, or had some well-known and honorable occupation.

By April 11, thirty-nine persons had been arrested in the North, and nineteen in the South. When the ship conveying them reached Santa Barbara, these latter were taken on board the "Guipuzcoana," which already had on board the men taken in the North. All were taken to San Blas. The evidence against the men was inconclusive, and most of them were permitted to return to California in a few months. It was reported that Graham and some others received compensation for their arrest and detention.

[128] In her interesting book, *Swinging the Censer*, 191–92, Katherine Bell refers to Nidever's marriage to Sinforosa Sanchez, a woman of good stock and closely connected with the Ortegas. Doña Rafaela Ortega Hill, Mrs. Bell's grandmother, was the baptismal sponsor of the first child of the Nidevers. Mrs. Nidever died in the year 1892, outliving her husband by nine years.

[129] John Wilson, a Scotch shipmaster and trader, probably arrived in California in 1826. The first original documentary record of him in California, according to Bancroft, was in 1826, when he was master of the "Thos. Nowlan." He was master of the "Avacucho," 1831–37; of the "Index," 1838–39, 1841–43; of the "Fly," 1840; and of the "Juanita" in 1844–45. Previous to 1836, he married Ramona Carrillo de Pacheco. From 1836 on, he considered Santa Barbara his home, and he was naturalized there in 1837. From 1839 to 1847, he was a partner of James Scott. There appears to be no record of the extent of his otter-hunting activities, other than references to his engagement in this occupation in 1841. With Scott, he was purchaser of the San Luis Obispo estate, and grantee of the ranchos, Cañada del Chorro and Cañada de los Osos, where he spent the rest of his life. He died in 1860.

Notes 113

[120] Like John Wilson, James Scott was a native of Scotland. He first visited California in 1826 as supercargo of the "Olive Branch" and the "Waverly." In 1827–28, he was master of the "Huascar." Though he was constantly on the move, and supercargo and master of various vessels, he seems to have considered Santa Barbara his home after 1830. He was an otter hunter at times, and from 1837 or earlier to 1847, a partner of John Wilson. He died in Santa Barbara in 1851.

[121] It seems that the property which came to be known as "Burton Mound," from its ownership later by Lewis Burton, was originally owned by James Burke (Don Santiago Burke). The second individual owner was Joseph Chapman (Don José Chatman). Although Nidever says he purchased the property from Chapman in 1849, there was a traditional owner or occupant, Thomas Robins, who was later a grantee of Hope ranch. There was subsequently another owner whose identity is in doubt. It is asserted by descendants that a Foxen owned the place a short time after Robins gave it up. Nidever sold the property to A. F. Hinchman, a Santa Barbara attorney, in 1850 or 1851.—John P. Harrington, *Exploration of the Burton Mound at Santa Barbara, California* (Washington, 1928), 57–58.

[122] John Coffin Jones, Jr., is put down as a California pioneer of 1830. A native of Boston, he was for some years a merchant in Honolulu, and at the same time, American consul at that port. For a number of years, he had large business transactions with California. Between 1830 and 1838, he visited this province as master or supercargo of his own vessels, the "Volunteer," "Louisa," "Harriet," "Blanchard," "Avon," "Bolivar," "Griffon," and "Rasselas."

He married Manuela, daughter of Carlos Carrillo, and in 1841 became a resident of Santa Barbara, though he continued to make visits to Honolulu. The marriage of Jones with Manuela Carrillo gave him his interest in the Island of Santa Rosa. This island was a land grant to Antonio and Carlos Carrillo for patriotic services, on October 4, 1843. On November 2, 1843, they conveyed and sold the island to Manuela Carrillo de Jones and Francisca Carrillo de Thompson. Possession of the island was given on December 2, 1843. Because of the ownership of the island by their wives, Jones and Thompson took an interest in stocking the island with a view to making profits from it. Jones's widow and Thompson and his children petitioned the United States Land Commissioners for recognition of their claim to ownership. The petition was denied by the Commissioners, but the United States courts reversed the decision of the Commissioners and awarded the island to the petitioners. See Ogden Hoffman, *Reports of Land Cases Determined in the United States District Court for the Northern District of California, June term, 1853, to June term, 1858, inclusive* (San Francisco, 1862), 17; *United States District Court, Southern District of California, No. 56 Docket, The United States vs. Manuela Carrillo de Jones et al., "Isla Santa Rosa,"* Transcript of the Record from the Board of Land Commissioners in Case No. 117, Filed August 30, 1854, W. H. Carter, Clerk.

In 1846, Jones sailed for Boston with his family. He died there a few years later.

[133] The companion of Nidever referred to as Breck was James Wm. Breck. The certain information about him is very meager. He was a Boston man who may have visited California on a whaler in 1829-30, and may have remained at that time. Some say that he came back from Honolulu in 1837 to become a permanent resident of Santa Barbara. His marriage took place in that city, and many children were born to him. He engaged in otter hunting between the years 1841 and 1845, but to what extent is not known. He is named as owner of a ranch in the vicinity of San Luis Obispo.

[134] The occasion for Micheltorena's march into southern California in 1845 was the unsettled political condition of the province. This condition resulted from division of authority, and ill feeling against the governor and the military forces by which he was supported. Many of his soldiers were liberated convicts, and the officers and regulars were of an undesirable character. The Californians called the soldiers *cholos*.

When trouble finally developed between Micheltorena and his opponents, his forces met those of the enemy in the territory between Salinas and Santa Clara. But there was no big fight; an agreement was made in December, under which Micheltorena was to send the *cholos* back to Mexico within three months. Instead of carrying out the agreement, the governor began enlisting foreigners under Sutter, Graham, and others, preparatory to striking his enemies a heavy blow. Alvarado and Castro, leaders in opposition to the governor, hastened south, took Los Angeles, and enlisted a force there. It was in connection with these events that Micheltorena passed through Santa Barbara, and endeavored, without success, to get Nidever and others to join him.

[135] Nidever must be in error in respect to the number of foreigners. Sutter started with a force of about 220 men, consisting of about 100 foreign riflemen under Captain Gantt, about 100 Indians under Ernest Rufus, 8 or 10 artillerymen, Dr. Townsend and John Sinclair as aides-de-camp, Jasper O'Farrell as quartermaster, S. J. Hensley as commissary, John Bidwell as secretary, and a few subordinate officers. After leaving Santa Barbara, 15 of Gantt's men were taken prisoner, 35 withdrew after this, and others had left the company previously. In spite of these defections and losses, some 50 of the foreign allies remained.—Bancroft, *California*, IV, 500-01; Wm. A. Streeter, *Recollections of Historic Events in California*, MS in Bancroft Collection, 35-51.

[136] The name of John Augustus Sutter is too well known in California history to require comment here. Just why he should join Micheltorena with a force does not appear in the records, but a study of his character would indicate that he thought business advantage lay in union with him.

[137] This was John Gantt, who came into California with the Chiles-Walker party in 1843. In 1844-45, his adventurous spirit led him to take up arms in Micheltorena's cause, or it may be that it was chance associations and not knowing which side to take in the conflict. He commanded the Mounted Rifle Company, which was part of Sutter's force of about 220 men. After the march south referred to by Nidever, the rifle company broke up and did not return in a body. Before leaving the south, Gantt

made a contract with Pico to attack Indian horse thieves for a share of the recovered livestock. It is probable that illness prevented his taking part in the difficulties of 1846-47. He died in the Napa Valley in 1849.

[138] "Their pilot," as Nidever designates William Knight, first came to California in 1841 from New Mexico with the Workman-Rowland party. He returned to New Mexico for his family in 1842, and, on his return to California in 1843, settled at what has since been known as Knight's Landing. He was naturalized in New Mexico, and was also married there to a native woman. Having lost his naturalization papers, he obtained a renewal of his naturalization in 1844. He was a prominent member of Gantt's company in the service of Micheltorena. Later he was active in the Bear Flag revolt, being one of its leaders in its early stages.

Soon after the discovery of gold, he established Knight's Ferry on the Stanislaus River. By some he is said to have been a man of culture, educated as a physician. But he was a person of rough ways, violent temper, and fighting spirit. When he died in 1849, he was supposed to be wealthy in money and lands. But his affairs were badly mixed up, and the wealth he was supposed to possess melted into thin air. His title to lands rested on the general title given to Sutter and a fraudulent grant from Pico. The petition of his heirs for confirmation of his title to lands was denied. See Tom Gregory, *History of Yolo County, California* (Historical Record Company, Los Angeles, California, 1913), 27-28.

[139] Ezekiel Merritt was another of the rough characters associated with Micheltorena's campaign. He was in California in 1841, and possibly earlier. In 1844, he appears to have been one of the party who threatened to release by force a Dr. Bale, who had got into trouble with the Vallejos and was in prison at Sonoma awaiting trial. As Nidever says, he was one of Sutter's men on the march south, being a member of Gantt's riflemen. He was prominently associated with the events leading up to the Bear Flag revolt. When Frémont went south, Merritt went with him, remaining with Gillespie at Los Angeles. Whether he died in the winter of 1847-48, or shortly after, is uncertain.

[140] Castro, with a force of perhaps 150 in all, left Los Angeles soon after February 1, 1846, and about a week later occupied San Buenaventura. His purpose in so doing was to watch the governor's movements and to prevent for a while his advance, while preparations were being made to defend Los Angeles against him. In the meantime, Micheltorena and Sutter started southward from Carpinteria. On learning that Castro had occupied San Buenaventura, they came back either to Carpinteria or to El Rincon, where they remained a week.

It was at this time that Lieutenant Coates and fifteen men of Gantt's company were captured while making a reconnaissance over the hills. Some suspect that the foreigners did not try very hard to keep from being captured. The prisoners were well treated in Castro's camp, and, on their promise to take no part in future hostilities, they induced a number of their companions to withdraw from Micheltorena's service. Wm. A. Streeter, in his *Recollections, loc. cit.*, says that, in spite of Captain Gantt's entreaties, thirty-five men, besides the paroled prisoners, decided to leave the company. Others had left previously, so that the foreign contingent was now reduced to not more than fifty, and many of these remained because of their unwillingness to abandon a cause after they had once espoused it.

[141] William Workman was an Englishman who came to California from New Mexico in 1841 with his family. He and John Rowland were the leaders of an immigrant party coming in that year. Political reasons influenced their leaving New Mexico: they were suspected of being concerned in a plot to embroil New Mexico in the Texan trouble. On their arrival in California, Rowland supplied the authorities with a list of his companions and a statement of their intention to comply with all legal requirements. Workman and Rowland secured the La Puente rancho, the title to which was confirmed by the Mexican authorities in 1845. With many others in the south, he was not favorable to Micheltorena and he did not trust Graham and Sutter. Fearing the bad feeling that would ensue if Micheltorena should succeed with the aid of foreigners, Workman led a company in opposition. In the early stages of the troubles of 1846-47, Workman was *comandante* of forces in opposition to Castro. He later acted as something of an intermediary between the American and Californian forces. In 1846, he and Hugo Perfecto Reid purchased for debt the mission of San Gabriel. In 1852, he was claimant for the Cajón de los Negros and Puente ranchos. He was a banker from about 1868, and, on the failure of his bank in 1876, committed suicide.

[142] John R. Rowland was a leader, with William Workman, of an immigrant party from New Mexico in 1841. He had lived in New Mexico eighteen years, married a native woman, and accumulated wealth. Like Workman, he left New Mexico under suspicion of complicity in filibustering schemes in connection with Texas. In spite of this, he was able to secure a grant of La Puente rancho along with Workman. Soon after this, he brought his family to the rancho, where he spent the rest of his life. He joined other prominent foreigners in opposition to Micheltorena. In 1846-47, Rowland was with the American forces. He was taken prisoner in the fight at the Chino rancho, but he was exchanged soon after. Of a retiring disposition, he took no part in public affairs in later years. His death occurred in 1873.

[143] The army of Micheltorena entered San Buenaventura on February 15 or 16, 1845. Castro retreated southward at once, possibly a few cannon shots being fired in his direction by Micheltorena's forces. After a day or two, Micheltorena pushed southward, arriving at Encino, in the San Fernando Valley, on February 19. By this time, Castro's forces had been reënforced by the forces under Alvarado and Pio Pico, and the Californians now numbered in all about four hundred men. There followed the so-called battle of Cahuenga, the capitulation of Micheltorena, and his agreement to leave the country.

[144] Wm. Fife, a native of Scotland, came to California in 1841. From 1845, and probably for several years earlier, he was an otter hunter at Santa Barbara. With the foreign residents of Santa Barbara, Fife was arrested in 1846, but, not being an American, he was released. After his

Notes

return from the mines, where he went in 1848, he resumed his otter hunting. He was murdered by a Sonoran at Santa Barbara in 1866.

[145] Redding McCoy, a native of New Jersey, was mate on the whaler "Dromo," from which he was discharged at Monterey in 1845. Aside from his connection with this vessel, and his experiences on the "Famer," nothing is known of him, except that he hunted otter and bear, that he possessed a lot in San Francisco in 1847, that he was at Bodega in 1848, and that he went to the mines.

[146] Graham H. Nye, a native of Massachusetts, may have visited the coast as early as 1830. Though several dates are given for his arrival, the first certain record shows him to have been on the coast in 1833-34 as master of the "Loriot," of which A. B. Thompson was supercargo. In 1847, he came on the "Guipuzcoana." There is much uncertainty about where he lived and what he did from that time until his death at St. Helena in 1878.

[147] "Charley Brown" was the name by which Carl Dittmann was known in California. Dittmann was a Prussian sailor who came to California on the "Euphemia" in 1844. He was one of the foreigners arrested in Santa Barbara in 1846, but he was released because he was not an American. For a number of years, he hunted sea otter with Nidever and others, an occupation interrupted by mining, 1848-50. His home was in Santa Barbara down to as late as 1878. He was companion of Nidever in his search for the Indian woman of San Nicolas Island, and was the man who first sighted the woman.

[148] Commodore Sloat sent the "Portsmouth" under Captain John B. Montgomery to Monterey in April, 1846, and the "Cyane" under Captain Mervine about the middle of May. Sloat, in the "Savannah," arrived at Monterey on July 2. On July 7, he went ashore with 250 men, raised the United States flag, and proclaimed California annexed to the United States.

Nidever's arrival was about one week after Sloat had raised the American flag. This is clear from his reference to the English warship. The ship referred to was the "Collingwood," commanded by Admiral Seymour. This vessel arrived on July 16, and sailed away on July 23. It would appear from this that Nidever arrived about July 16. He says he remained two or three days. This is probably correct, for he does not mention the arrival of Frémont, which was on July 19. For some detail on these events, see Lieutenant Fred Walpole, *Four Years in the Pacific*, II (London, 1849), 204-19; *Niles' Register*, LXXI, 133; Walter Colton, *Dock and Port* (New York, 1860), 390-91.

[149] It appears that when Nidever returned to Monterey, Frémont and Stockton had made conquest of the south and returned to Monterey. On the way south, Frémont had stopped at Santa Barbara, where he left a small garrison. An uprising in the south soon drove Gillespie's small United States garrison out of Los Angeles, and the few men under Lieutenant Talbot out of Santa Barbara. When Talbot and his small company reached Monterey on November 8, Nidever had evidently left for the south. Streeter, *Recollections, op. cit.*, 55-63, gives a detailed story of Talbot's escape from Santa Barbara with his men.

[150] Totoi Pico, as he was familiarly known, or José de Jesús Pico, his real name, had been prominent in the San Luis Obispo region for some years, where he was grantee of the Piedra Blanco rancho in 1840, and administrator of San Miguel Mission, 1841-43. He took part in the movement against Micheltorena, and he was later a captain, under General Castro and Governor Pico, in the forces resisting the Americans. After the taking of Los Angeles by Frémont and Stockton, Castro's men started in several parties for their northern homes. Some of these were captured on the way by a detachment of the California battalion and paroled. Among these was José de Jesús Pico.

When the Californians rose against the Americans, Pico broke his parole, as did many other Californians, and joined the army under Manuel Castro, who was commandant of military operations in the north, with headquarters at San Luis Obispo. He was on good terms with Wilson and Scott, who, if not active on either side, were regarded as not friendly to the Americans. When Frémont marched south, Pico was taken prisoner at Wilson's rancho. On December 16, he was sentenced by court martial to be shot. As a result of the tearful pleadings of Pico's wife and their fourteen children, together with solicitations by some officers of Frémont's, whom Pico had befriended in former years, Frémont pardoned Pico. Pico then joined Frémont, and on the journey south he rendered every aid possible. These events must have taken place just about the time of Nidever's arrival, but whether they occurred before or after, there is no way of knowing for certain.

[151] Antonio María Ortega had been prominent in Mexican provincial affairs for some years. In 1827-28, he was a member of the territorial *Diputación*. He received the grant of the Refugio rancho in 1834, and his claim for it was approved by the United States. His name was proposed for subprefect on the resignation of Raimundo Carrillo in 1841. At the time of Nidever's arrival from the north in 1846, Ortega was *alcalde*.

[152] Raimundo Carrillo, at the time Nidever arrived from the north in 1846, was *comandante* at Santa Barbara under Flores. From here, on November 30, he ordered Janssens to go to San Luis Obispo and learn what force was there, if proper precautions had been taken, and if there was any news of Frémont's movements.—Don Agustín Janssens, *Documentos para la Historia de California* (MS in Bancroft Library), 56–57. He evidently got out of Santa Barbara on the approach of Frémont, for he offered no resistance to him, but came from San Buenaventura to join another force opposing him. Previous to this, he had held numerous offices, and subsequently, in 1849, he was *alcalde*.

[153] An account of the trip down the coast similar in content to Nidever's, but much more in detail, is given by Carl Dittmann, otherwise known as Charley Brown, who, on this trip, had charge of a large surfboat in which they carried supplies.—See Carl Dittmann, *Narrative of a Seafaring Life on the Coast of California* (MS in Bancroft Library), 27–37.

[154] After the small United States force had been driven out of Santa Barbara, American residents were arrested. Some of these were sent to Los Angeles, and some were paroled. Carl Dittmann (Charley Brown),

who had charge of one of the boats with Nidever, says: "When we reached the shore we found six men [Californians] waiting for us, who barely gave time to land, before they arrested us. The Capt., Bill Fife and I were at once taken up to Raymundo Carrillo's house and their [sic] asked our nationality. Fife, being a Scotchman, and I a German we were allowed to go, with the instruction that if we wished to leave town we must get a passport. We told them that we had no desire to leave the place, but proposed making our stay here during the winter as had been our wont. The Capt. was told that he would have to go to L. A. a prisoner, as the other Americans had gone. He said that he wished to remain here with his family, and did not want to be disturbed. They told him that he must go to L. A. since he was an American and that if he would not go alone he should be sent under guard. He promised them that he would go alone, but instead of going he went out into foothills near Montecito, where he remained until Frémont came, and then joined him. About the same time that Capt. Nidever was ordered to go to Los Angeles, several Americans were arrested and taken down there and among them Capt. A. B. Thompson. He hired me to take charge of his house, which I did until his brother came out about a month after."—Dittmann, *op. cit.*, 37–39. Streeter, *op. cit.*, 65–75, gives many details of these arrests.

[155] In 1846, José de la Guerra y Noriega was an old man, having been born in Spain in 1779. He had held office under Spain and then under Mexico, almost continuously from 1801 until 1842, when he retired from military service. Bancroft says of him with respect to the troubles of 1846–47: "Though not friendly to the United States, he kept quiet for the most part, and did not indulge in any offensive partisanship." Some of his acts may be justly condemned, but it would have been difficult for any person to pass through the changes of his day without giving greater cause for offense. Until his death in 1858, he lived quietly in Santa Barbara.

[156] Francisco de la Guerra was the son of Captain José de la Guerra y Noriega. Between 1840 and the American occupation, he held political offices, but he never attained any special prominence. He was more or less openly hostile to the United States, but he became a loyal citizen of the United States when its authority had been finally established, and he held the office of mayor of Santa Barbara for several years after 1851.

[157] José Vicente Ortega was a son of José María Ortega, officer at Santa Barbara and owner of Refugio rancho.

[158] In the contest between the United States and Mexico for possession of California in 1846–47, Thomas O. Larkin, who had been a successful merchant in California since 1832, and United States consul from 1843, found himself the victim of the unwisdom of others. He knew that California was but slightly attached to Mexico, and he was convinced that, either in the event of war with Mexico, or by purchase, the people of California and local rulers might be induced peaceably to transfer their allegiance to the United States. He was commissioned by the United States to bring about this result, and he was making progress in that direction when Frémont's activities in California, followed by the Bear Flag revolt, defeated his plans.

As a result, bitterness and war came in the accomplishment of what might otherwise have been brought about amicably. Then, in the midst of the conflict which might have been avoided, he was taken prisoner while on his way to San Francisco to visit his sick daughter. As a prisoner of Manuel Castro, he saw the battle of Natividad, after which he was carried south to be held as a prisoner until the end of hostilities. He passed through Santa Barbara while Nidever was in hiding. It should be said that Larkin was kindly treated at the time of his capture and afterward, the Californians having no ill feeling toward him.

[159] When news reached Monterey of uprisings in the south, preparations were made for reconquest. On November 17, Frémont left Monterey and in a few days united his forces at San Juan, where he remained until the end of November. After the organization of his battalion was completed, on November 29 he started south to coöperate with Stockton against General Flores.

The route of Frémont was up the San Benito, over the mountain to the Salinas, then up that valley to San Miguel, and then on to San Luis Obispo. After three days here, during which the capture, trial, and parole of Totoi Pico took place (see fn. 150, *supra*), the battalion left on December 17.

As Frémont approached the mountains, Benjamin Foxen, at whose ranch he camped, and others warned him of danger of attack by the Californians, whose strength in men, horses, and weapons was greatly exaggerated. Particularly, he was warned of a plan to trap him in the narrow defile of Gaviota, there to attack him by rolling rocks down from the precipice above. Whatever danger there was at Gaviota was avoided by taking the more difficult route over San Marcos Pass, in the crossing of which many dangers and hardships were encountered. But they met no resistance by a hostile force, not even at Santa Barbara, which was reached on November 27.—John Bidwell, *California*, 1841–48 (MS), 201–04; Patrick McChristian, *Narrative*, 5–8; *Santa Cruz Sentinel*, March 21, 1868; and Janssens, *Vida y Aventuras en California* (MS), 193–95.

Streeter, *Recollections*, *op. cit.*, 75–81, gives some details of Frémont's approach to Santa Barbara. According to his story, he, in company with Burton and Sparks, rode out and met Frémont at the foot of the mountains on the Santa Barbara side of the pass. Frémont told him, when they met, that he intended to enter Santa Barbara with fire and sword, and that, with the exception of one or two buildings, he did not intend to leave a single building in the town, because all the Californians were against him. Streeter says that he assured Frémont that the Californians were out against him because they had to be, and that, if he would spare the town, he [Streeter] would send word to many who would return in a few days. This course was accordingly followed, and numbers of bands came in and signed the parole.

[160] Caesareo Lataillade, a Spaniard of French descent, came to California in 1842 as supercargo of the Mexican trading vessel "Trinidad." He made Santa Barbara his home, and here married María Antonia de la Guerra. His name appears prominently in business and official communi-

cations from the time of his arrival until his death in 1849, when he accidentally shot himself.

[161] Carl Dittmann, in his *Narrative, op. cit.*, 41, says: "Capt. Nidever and Mr. Sparks joined Frémont here. A hunter by the name of Halstead who went up with us and joined Frémont at Monterey, tried to get me to join here but I did not care to."

[162] Nidever is evidently in error in saying that the "Collingwood" was at Monterey when he stopped there on the way south, for it left on July 23, and there appears no record of its return. He may be thinking of encounters in July on his way north.

There probably was a shooting contest when the stop was made on the way south, for Carl Dittmann, otherwise known as Charley Brown, who was with Nidever, in connection with the trip south says: "At Monterey we went into camp on the point just above the Town. While here we were visited by officers from several men-of-war then at anchor in the harbor. They bought a few skins from us. At a target match that was gotten up from among Fremont's men to show the Naval officers some good shooting, our Capt. Geo. Nidever was asked to join them and he did better shooting than all of them."—Dittmann, *op. cit.*, 26-27. It will be noted that he mentions no English ships or officers.

William F. Swasey, consular secretary to Larkin, makes mention of a contest of shooting skill between Frémont's men and officers of the "Collingwood," but when this took place, or whether Nidever was a contestant, does not appear, so the confusion is not cleared. See William F. Swasey, *California, 1845-46* (MS in Bancroft Library), 13-14.

[163] This was Julius Martin, who with his wife and three children came to California in 1843 with the Chiles-Walker party, and established his family in the Gilroy region. For several years he worked at different places, but Gilroy was his home. He served under Frémont and Fauntleroy in 1846.

[164] Stockton and Kearny had already taken Los Angeles. With Frémont occupying the San Fernando Valley, the situation of the Californians was hopeless. Jesús Pico, who had accompanied Frémont after Frémont had spared his life, was sent as a messenger to the Californians. The treaty drawn up was known as the Cahuenga Treaty because the articles of capitulation were drawn up and signed at the old Cahuenga ranch house, which Frémont used as headquarters. When Frémont and Andrés Pico put their signatures to this conciliatory document on January 13, 1847, the war was over in California.

[165] This refers to the sale of the Burton Mound property.

[166] This was, of course, the sale of the interests on the island and not of the island itself, which is public domain and not private property.

[167] See *supra*, 37-39, for Nidever's statement telling how it happened that the Indian woman whose rescue he is about to describe came to be on the Island of San Nicolas. Nidever's story and Dittmann's shorter one are the only original narratives of the episode of the finding of the Indian woman.

In *Scribner's Monthly*, September, 1880, Mrs. Emma C. Hardacre published an article, "Eighteen Years Alone," which tells much the same story as Nidever gives. She interviewed Nidever, Dittmann, Dr. Brinkerhoff, and others, so that her story has some of the qualities of original material. Mrs. Hardacre's account is marred somewhat for historical purposes by subjectivity of treatment and ornateness of style, but it should be read along with the Nidever and Dittman documents in order to get, as nearly as possible, a correct picture of what actually occurred.

[168] It is stated by Mrs. Hardacre, who received the story from Thomas Jeffries, that the Mission Fathers, as late as 1850, believed it quite possible that the Indian woman and child who had been left on the island were still alive, and that Father González Rubio offered Jeffries two hundred dollars if he would cross the channel and find the woman. She says he made the trip in midwinter of 1850–51 but had no success. See Hardacre, *op. cit.*, 659. Father Engelhardt accepts such evidence of a trip as authentic. See Engelhardt, *Santa Barbara Mission* (San Francisco, 1923), 449–52.

[169] San Nicolas Island is about seventy miles from the mainland in almost a direct line south from Santa Barbara. The island is eight miles long and three and one-half miles wide. It is today dry, sterile, and windswept. See Davidson, *United States Coast and Geodetic Survey* (Washington, 1863), 21.

[170] Father Engelhardt, after telling the story of the woman, remarks: "It was also claimed that Juana Maria after her death found her resting place in the cemetery of Santa Barbara mission. . . ." Then he says: "Were it not that Mr. Nidever's fame for veracity appears above suspicion, we should declare the whole story a myth, for the reason that, after a close examination of the Baptismal Registers at the Mission and at the Parish Church of Santa Barbara, we failed to discover any entry recording the woman's Baptism in either the Mission or the Parish Church. Likewise, there is no record noted of her burial in the Mission Cemetery."—Engelhardt, *The Santa Barbara Mission* (San Francisco, 1923), 449–52.

In a conversation with Father Engelhardt in May, 1932, the editor asked the Mission historian if there were any further light on the question of the baptism and burial of the Indian woman. He said he knew of none, but that he would reëxamine the Mission records. In a letter from him to William H. Ellison, May 14, 1932, he says: "The Baptismal Register from 1851 to 1858 has no Juana Maria entered by Fr. Sanchez or anyone else. . . . I believe it will never be cleared up, as there is no document extant in our archives. . . ."

Perhaps some weight should be given to the words of Mrs. Hardacre (*op. cit.*, 664) written in 1880: "In a walled cemetery, from whose portals gleam ghastly skull and cross-bones, close to the Santa Barbara Mission, under the shelter of the tower, is the neglected grave of a devoted mother, the heroine of San Nicolas." Basing their action on this and other traditional stories, in 1928 the Santa Barbara Chapter of the D.A.R. placed on the mission wall beneath the tower, a tablet in memory of the unknown mother and to mark her grave, and the tablet was accepted by Father Augustine on behalf of the Padres.

BIBLIOGRAPHY

Arkansas Gazette, November 2, 1831.

BAKER, D. W. C.
A Texas Scrap Book. A. S. Barnes, New York, Chicago, and New Orleans, c1875.

BANCROFT, HUBERT HOWE
History of California. II and III, San Francisco, 1885; IV and V, San Francisco, 1886.
Literary Industries. San Francisco, 1890.
History of Nevada, Colorado, and Wyoming. San Francisco, 1890.
History of North Mexican States and Texas. II, San Francisco, 1889.

BARKER, EUGENE C.
"The Government of Austin's Colony, 1821–1831," *The Southwestern Historical Quarterly*, January, 1918.

BEECHEY, F. W.
Narrative of a Voyage to the Pacific and Bering's Strait to Coöperate with the Polar Expeditions: Performed in His Majesty's Ship Blossom Under the Command of Captain F. W. Beechey, F. R. S., etc., in the Years 1825, 1826, 1827, 1828. Published by authority of the Lord's Commissioners of the Admiralty, Philadelphia, 1832.

BELL, KATHERINE M.
Swinging the Censer. Findlay Press, Hartford, Conn., 1931.

BIDWELL, JOHN
California, 1841–48. MS in Bancroft Library.

BOLTON, HERBERT E., ED.
Spanish Explorations in the Southwest. Scribners, New York, 1916.

BUNNELL, L. H.
Discovery of Yosemite. 1880.

CABALLERIA Y COLLELL, JUAN
History of Santa Barbara, California, from Its Discovery to Our Own Day. Translated by EDMUND BURKE. Santa Barbara, 1892.

CAMP, CHARLES L.
"The Chronicles of George Yount," *California Historical Society Quarterly*, II, 3–66.

CHAPMAN, CHARLES E.
A History of California: The Spanish Period. Macmillan, New York, 1923.

CHITTENDEN, HENRY M.
The American Fur Trade of the Far West: A History of the Pioneer Trading Posts and Early Fur Companies of the Missouri Valley and the Rocky Mountains and of the Overland Commerce with Santa Fe. 3 vols. F. P. Harper, New York, 1902.

CLELAND, ROBERT G.
　A History of California: The American Period. Macmillan, New York, 1922.

COLTON, WALTER
　Deck and Port. D. W. Evans and Company, New York, 1860.

DAVIDSON, GEORGE C.
　United States Coast and Geodetic Survey. Washington, D. C., 1863.
　United States Coast and Geodetic Survey; Appendix No. 7, Report for 1886. Washington, D. C., 1887.

DITTMANN, CARL
　Narrative of a Seafaring Life on the Coast of California. MS in Bancroft Library, 1878.

DYE, JOB F.
　Recollections of California Since 1832. MS, 22 pages, in Bancroft Library, 1877.

ENGELHARDT, FR. ZEPHYRIN
　Santa Barbara Mission. James H. Barry Company, San Francisco, 1923.

FOWLER, JACOB
　Journal . . . 1821-2. Edited by ELLIOTT COUES. New York, 1898.

FRANCHERE, GABRIEL
　"Narrative of a Voyage to the Northwest Coast of America," in Thwaites, *Early Western Travels,* VI, New York, 1854.

GIDNEY, C. M., et al.
　History of Santa Barbara, San Luis Obispo, and Ventura Counties, California. Lewis Publishing Company, Chicago, 1917.

GITTINGER, ROY
　The Formation of the State of Oklahoma. University of California Press, Berkeley, 1917.

GREGORY, THOMAS J.
　History of Yolo County, California. Historic Record Company, Los Angeles, 1913.

HARDACRE, EMMA C.
　"Eighteen Years Alone," *Scribner's Monthly,* XX, 657-64, September, 1880.

HARRINGTON, JOHN P.
　Exploration of the Burton Mound at Santa Barbara. United States Government Printing Office, Washington, D. C., 1928.

HEMPSTEAD, FAY
　History of the State of Arkansas. F. F. Hansell and Brother, c1889.

HILL, LUTHER B.
　A History of Oklahoma. I. Lewis Publishing Company, Chicago and New York, 1906.

HODGE, FREDERICK W., ED.
   Handbook of American Indians North of Mexico. 2 vols. Washington, D. C., 1907–10.
IRVING, WASHINGTON
   A Tour of the Prairies. J. Murray, London, 1835.
   Adventures of Captain Bonneville, U. S. A., in the Rocky Mountains and Far West. Digested from his *Journal* and Illustrated from Various Other Sources. G. P. Putnam and Sons, New York, 1868.
JANSSENS, DON AGUSTÍN
   Documentos para la Historia de California. MS in Bancroft Library.
LANCEY, THOMAS
   Cruise of the Dale: Scraps from the *San José Pioneer.* Bancroft Library.
LEONARD, ZENAS
   Narrative of the Adventures of Zenas Leonard. Printed and published by D. W. Moore, Clearfield, Pa., 1839. (Copy in possession of James Leonard, Santa Barbara, California.)
   Leonard's Narrative: Adventures of Zenas Leonard (Clearfield, Pa., 1839), *Fur-trader and Trapper, 1831–1836.* Reprinted from the rare original of 1839, and edited by W. F. WAGNER. The Burrows Brothers Company, Cleveland, 1904.
MCCHRISTIAN, PATRICK
   Narrative. MS in Bancroft Library.
MEEK, STEPHEN H. L.
   Item in *Jonesborough* (Tenn.) *Sentinel,* March 8, 1837. Reprinted in *Niles' Register,* Vol. LII, March 25, 1837.
PHELPS, WILLIAM D.
   Fore and Aft, or Leaves from the Life of an Old Sailor. Nichols and Hall, Boston, 1871.
RUSSELL, CARL PARCHER
   One Hundred Years in Yosemite. Stanford University Press, 1931.
Santa Cruz Sentinel, June 14, 1873.
SCHOONOVER, T. J.
   The Life and Times of General John A. Sutter. Bullock-Carpenter Company, Sacramento, 1907.
STORKE, YDA ADDIS
   A Memorial and Biographical History of the Counties of Santa Barbara, San Luis Obispo, and Ventura, California. Chicago, 1871.
STREETER, WM. A.
   Recollections of Historical Events in California, 1843–1878. MS in Bancroft Library.
SWASEY, WILLIAM F.
   California, 1845–6. MS in Bancroft Library.
VICTOR, FRANCES FULLER
   River of the West. Hartford, Conn., and Toledo, O., 1870.

WAGNER, W. F., editor. See under Leonard, Zenas.

WALPOLE, LIEUT. FRED
Four Years in the Pacific, II. London, 1849.

WHITE, JOSEPH M.
A New Collection of Laws, Charters, and Local Ordinances of the Governments of Great Britain, France, and Spain, Relating to the Concessions of Land in Their Respective Countries; together with the Laws of Mexico and Texas on the Same Subject. I, Philadelphia, 1839.

WYETH, JOHN B.
Oregon, or a Short History of a Long Journey, in Thwaites, *Early Western Travels*, XXI. Cleveland, 1905.

ZAVALISHIN, DIMITRY
Russian Affairs. V. The Affairs of the Ross Colony. Moscow, 1866. Translated by Mr. KLINHOFSTROM. (MS of the translation is in Bancroft Library.)

INDEX

Alvarado, Juan Bautista, 46, 47, 48–49, 55
Arapahoes, 11 ff., 14, 16, 18, 21
Bean, Colonel, vii, viii, 4, 6–7, 9, 13, 19, 37
Black Steward (Allen Light), 39–40, 41, 43, 46, 47, 48, 54, 55, 57, 62
Blackfeet Indians, viii, 26, 27–29
Breck, James W., 58, 59 *passim*, 63
Brown, Charley (Carl Dittmann), 60, 61, 63, 64, 74, 78, 80, 81, 82, 84, 86
Burton, Lewis T., 36, 37, 58, 75
Carrillo, Don Carlos: his party, 47
Carrillo, Raymundo (or Raimundo), 64, 65, 67–68
Cherokee Indians, vii, 1, 3, 4
Comanches, 7, 8–9
Craig, Dr. James, 15, 19, 20
Crow Indians, 22, 30, 31
Denny (Dana), Capt. W. G., license arrangements with, 36, 40, 46; land plans made by, 49
Dittmann, Carl. *See* Charley Brown
Dye, Job F., 15, 37, 59
Fife, William, 60, 61, 63, 64, 73
Frapp (Fraeb), Henry, 25, 26, 28, 29, 30
Frémont, ix, 63, 65, 68, 69, 70, 71 *passim*, 72, 73
Gant (Gantt), John, 36, 59
Guadalupe Hidalgo, treaty of, x
Graham, Isaac, 7, 10, 11, 12, 15, 16, 20, 21, 46, 55, 59
Green River Valley, trappers' rendezvous in, 31–32
Guerra, Anto[nio] Ma[ría] de la, 68, 69
Guerra, Capt. Francisco de la, 65, 67, 68, 69
Guerra, José de la, 65
Hewitt, George, 55 *passim*, 58, 59
Horses, capturing wild, 14
Indian child, rescue of, 35
Indian woman, finding and removal of, from San Nicolas Island, 81–89
Jeffries, Tom, 77, 79, 80
Larkin, Thomas O., 66
Lataillade, Cesareo, 68, 69
Light, Allen. *See* Black Steward

McCoy, Redding, 60, 61 *passim*, 62, 73–74
Mexicans: and Arapahoes deadly enemies, 18; hospitality of, 19
Micheltorena, 59, 60 *passim*
Nale (Naile), Henry, 20, 55
Nidever, George: a symbolic figure, x; birth and early life of, 1 ff.; built a raft with Sinclair, 3–4; joined party of trappers and hunters, 4; shooting ability of, 4–5; hunting and Indian fighting of, 8 ff.; Mexican hospitality described by, 18–19; arrival of, at Pierre's Hole, 24, and departure of, 26; encounter of, with Blackfeet Indians, 27–29; decided to go to California, 31–32; joined Capt. Walker's company, 32; arrival of, in California, 34; finding of Indian child by, 35; joined Alvarado's forces, 46–47; search of, for suitable location for ranch, 48, 55; adventures of, with grizzlies, 49 ff.; otter hunt by, on Lower California coast, 55 ff.; marriage of, 58; arrest of, 65 ff.; search for, at his home, 68; shooting contest, 71; gold-digging experiences of, 75; purchase and sale of San Miguel Island by, 76–77; finding of footprints on San Nicolas Island, 77, 81, and finding of Indian woman by party of, 81 ff.
Nidever, Mark, 7, 10, 15; killed by Indians, 16–17
Northwestern Indians, 37, 38; tactics of, 40–43; defeat of, 44, 45; as otter hunters, 44–45
O'Brien, John, 40, 42, 43, 75
Ortega, Anto. Ma., *alcalde*, 64
Ortega, Vicente, 66
Pawnee Indians, 10, 12, 14
Pico, Andrés, 73
Pico, Totoi, 63, 70
Pierre's Hole: a trappers' rendezvous, 24 ff.; center of a rich beaver country, 25
Robinson, Alfred, 36, 56
Rocha, Juan José, 47 *passim*

[127]

Rowland, John R., 20-21, 60
San Fernando, N. M.: trading posts at, 13, 19; prices paid for skins at, 22
San Nicolas Island: removal of Indians from, 37; piles of human bones on, 44; finding of footprints on, 77, 81; finding of Indian woman on, 82 ff.
Santa Rosa Island: hunting on, 36, 39; people on, in 1836, 40; tactics of Northwestern Indians near, 40-44
Sanchez, Sinforosa, 58
Simmonds, Stephen, 48, 54, 62
Sinclair, Alex., vii, viii, 3, 4, 5, 10, 13; made leader, 14, 20, 21; shot by Indians, 27; brother of, with Frémont, 71
Snake Indians, 22, 30, 44

Stockton, Commodore, 70, 73
Sublette, Milton, 25
Sublette, William, 24, 25; elected leader, 27
Sutter, John Augustus, 59
Sparks, Isaac, 36, 37, 39, 40, 44, 45, 46, 49, 52, 55 *passim*, 56, 58, 59 *passim*, 62, 63, 69-70, 73, 75
Thompson, Capt. A. B., 36, 45, 46, 59, 60, 61
Valle, Don Ign[aci]o del, 47
Walker, Capt. Joseph R., viii, 32, 34, 75
Wasner Ranch, 48, 55
Wilson, Capt. John, 58, 61
Workman, William, 20-21, 60
Wyatt's company of emigrants, 25, 26, 30
Young, Capt. Ewing, 20
Yount, George C., viii, 34, 35-36

www.ingramcontent.com/pod-product-compliance
Lightning Source LLC
Chambersburg PA
CBHW021712230426
43668CB00008B/810